John
Ormond

Collected Poems

John Ormond

Collected Poems

Edited by Rian Evans

Introduction by Patrick McGuinness

SEREN

Seren is the book imprint of
Poetry Wales Press Ltd,
57 Nolton Street, Bridgend, Wales, CF31 3AE

**Explore thirty years of fine writing at
www.serenbooks.com**

First published 2015

Selection and editorial apparatus © Rian Evans, 2015
Poems © the Estate of John Ormond, 2015

Introduction copyright Patrick McGuinness

The rights of the above mentioned to be identified as
the authors of this work have been asserted in accordance
with the Copyright, Design and Patents Act.

ISBN: 978-1-85411-521-8

A CIP record for this title is available from the British Library.

The publisher acknowledges the financial assistance of the
Welsh Books Council.

Printed by CPI Group (UK) Ltd, Croydon

Contents

II
Saturday Pictures

III
Cathedral Builders

Certain Episodes Reported with No Offence Meant to God

Foreword

When seeing my father's Gregynog collection *Cathedral Builders* through the press following his death in 1990, I was conscious of fulfilling a duty, completing a project which had meant a great deal to him. Almost 25 years on, the present undertaking has a different sense of obligation. For, though the Gregynog title-poem may be well-known – a Poetry Please favourite – and while other Ormond poems have been frequently anthologised, his work has not been readily available. In that sense, this volume – rather like the library-reminders that used to arrive through the post – is long overdue. Accordingly, I have taken the opportunity to bring together a more extensive collection of his poems than has hitherto appeared; many will be read for the first time since their original publication.

Whether he would have thanked me for this is a moot point. He was reticent and mostly self-deprecating about the early poetry, yet his punctilious approach when documenting the lives of others would, I hope, have permitted him to accept that, over time, it might be useful to look at the whole span of his own output. He had been adamant, however, that no poem he himself had not sanctioned for publication should appear after his death and I have honoured that wish here.

Ormond was 19 years old when a poem of his was published in the magazine *Poetry Quarterly* and newly come of age by the time of his inclusion in the anthology of *Modern Welsh Poetry*, edited for Faber by Keidrych Rhys and published in 1944. Rhys placed his poets alphabetically and, under the name Ormond Thomas – he would not drop the family name until a decade later – his poems sit between those of Dylan Thomas and of R.S. Thomas. However satisfying such a juxtaposition might seem, in fact, Ormond's early success would weigh on him as somehow too easily gained. He even destroyed much he'd written in a ritual burning. Yet, in the collections he eventually published, he did include work from the 40s and 50s, perhaps finally accepting that the poet he had once been and the poet he had become sprang from the same instinctive commitment.

In his various selections, Ormond's preference for broadly thematic sequencing meant that the order in which he placed the poems did not correspond to that in which they had been written. This was not always perceived to be helpful and occasionally led to misassumptions. Hence my decision to put the poems in chronological order in this volume, with a section for each of the five decades in which they were written and details of a poem's first publication appearing in the following notes. In many instances, unequivocal dating was not possible. But where there was evidence of the conception of a poem dating from a particular time well before its eventual publication, I opted to place it earlier so as to give a sense of the sequence and development of ideas.

The decision to include some of the verses written for the *News Chronicle* in the mid-1950s stems from a similar premise, not least since they date from a time until now mainly viewed as though it had been barren. Much has been made of Vernon Watkins's advice "not to publish any further collection until he was thirty" and Ormond himself referred to his "long silence", apparently disinclined to count the *News Chronicle* verses as poetry. Yet, the simplicity and clarity he sometimes achieved in them suggests that, in their way, they too are part of the overall picture.

My purpose then is not so much to make claims for his work, which have in any case been made elsewhere, but rather to put it in historical context and to allow his parallel pursuits as a film-maker to be seen as part of his poetical perspective. Ormond's output was never going to be vast, he was too self-critical for that. Added together, though, it amounts to more than has sometimes been assumed. And, while his death at 67 may well have deprived us of the further late flowering his writing in the 80s seemed to promise, I find it salutary to reflect on the life-force that allowed him to survive early childhood at all. Many were the vigils at his bedside when he twice endured rheumatic fever, antibiotics not yet known. He was always happy to suggest that the pleasure he found in words was part of his cure.

Rian Evans
2015

Introduction

On January 25, 1947, Lynette Roberts noted in her *Carmarthenshire Diary*: 'Sometime ago, John Ormond Thomas again came to see us. It was his second visit. When we first met him he was studying at the university. He was now working for the *Picture Post*. He had come [...] to write up a stern protest that was being sponsored by all parties against the land-grabbing habit of the War Office. This was published today as a first article in *Picture Post*.'

Roberts and her husband Keidrych Rhys were living in the village of Llanybri. Rhys was the editor of the international magazine *Wales* and of the anthologies *Poems from the Forces* (1941) and *Modern Welsh Poetry* (1944). From this geographically remote but culturally central West Wales base, Rhys played an energetic role in the promotion of Welsh writing in English. Apart from Dylan Thomas, Keidrych's close friend and best man at his wedding to Lynette, Rhys and Roberts's visitors included the young R.S. Thomas, Ernest Rhys, Alun Lewis, Glyn Jones, Vernon Watkins and others. *Wales* magazine, meanwhile, published writers as diverse as John Betjeman, Kafka, Robert Graves and both Thomases. In the 1 July 1943 issue, the poem 'Procession' by a 20 year-old Ormond – his name appearing as Ormond Thomas – shared pages with, among others, Vernon Watkins, Alun Lewis and William Empson. The following year, Rhys went on to publish three of his poems, among them 'Poem in February' in *Modern Welsh Poetry*.

Like many young poets in Wales and beyond, Ormond Thomas began writing in the crowded shadow of Dylan Thomas, his senior by almost ten years. This was the time of the 'New Romantics' and the 'Apocalypse' poets, writers such as J.F. Hendry, Henry Treece, Nicholas Moore, who, liberated by (and also chained to) the example of Thomas, strove (as Hendry put it in his introduction to the *The New Apocalypse* anthology of 1939) to 'write organically'. Hendry and Treece and their loose group were reacting against the genera-tion of Auden and MacNeice and Spender. They in turn were reacted against by The Movement, the (again loose) group that emerged in the 1950s to reinstall a poetry of form and thought and rationality. As Robert Conquest claimed in the first *New Lines* anthology (1956), the poetry of the 1940s suffered from an excess of the 'Id'. Literary history has been unkind to the poets of the 'forties, a judgment endorsed by the attitude of many of the poets themselves to their earliest work: Norman MacCaig famously dismissed his 1940s poetry as a 'vomitorium of images', and disowned it in what he called a 'long haul back to lucidity'. And yet reaction is a shaping force; we are made by what we escape from as much as what we escape to. Though he did not properly meet him until June 1946, in the context of a *Picture Post* profile article, Ormond had been in contact with Dylan Thomas by letter, and his early work shows the almost inevitable imprint of Thomas's influence.

What is important about the way in which young Welsh poets responded to Thomas by comparison with, say, the English or the Scottish poets, is the relative moderation of their excess. With Ormond Thomas, as with contemporaries and near-contemporaries such as Lynette Roberts, Vernon Watkins, Leslie Norris (another poet who underplayed his 'forties work), Glyn Jones and others, the Dylanesque high style is certainly there, but in a more muted form than in, say, Hendry or Treece or even the early W.S. Graham. We might attribute this to mere coincidence (they happen in literature too), but we might also consider how the Welsh poets' acquaintance with Welsh-language verse, and in particular the strict-metre forms they knew or had studied, enabled them to tamp down their loquaciousness, to introduce – as in Dylan Thomas himself – something tightly-sprung and economical beneath the associative scatterings of the 'id'. This facet of Thomas's work accounts for something in his work that nobody, least of all his imitators, seemed able to replicate: that sense of the poems being precise even when incomprehensible (this is, incidentally, the only way in which Thomas may meaningfully be compared with Rimbaud).

In a contribution to *Artists in Wales 2*, published in 1974, a year after the appearance of his collection *Definition of a Waterfall* from Oxford University Press, Ormond recalled his debt to the Welsh *cynghanedd* and his attempts, in the early 1940s, to assimilate some of its rules:

I tried to write second and third lines based upon similar consonantal systems and those constructions were meant to be read with the eye, three lines, say, being read simultaneously, rather like a musical score.

This tradition, most visibly grafted onto English poetry by Gerard Manley Hopkins, goes some way towards explaining why the poetry produced by many of the young Anglo-Welsh writers differs, in its culture-specific particularity, from that of their Scottish and English contemporaries. It may not, of course, be any better, but it has a context, and a grounding in craft, that distinguishes it and roots in time and place and affinity. Ormond's earliest poems are in this sense a product of more than just the ambient Dylanism of the time, though they certainly owe a great deal to that ambiance. Add to this the extraordinary attention Thomas's persona helped to train on the literature and culture of Wales, and we see how the 'Rimbaud of Cwmdonkin Drive' might hinder his contemporaries as much as he might help them. When, in a 1989 interview, Ormond told Richard Poole that Dylan 'infected people with the power, musically especially, of language. [...] The bad thing was the obscurantist side of Dylan', he was speaking for a generation of poets who, in reckoning with Thomas, were also reckoning with their younger selves.

'Birthday Poem', first published in 1944, is Ormond's gift to his future wife, Glenys: 'I give you for your birthday night/ a poem to lay your head upon' reads its dedication:

Dream softly, as the waterfall
darkly descends, of the remotest
moments, dim in their beginnings, lit
by the nearest sunlight in the green
rocks of water, purple weeds
under the cave and hill
of happiness.

The dream state is likened to a waterfall, and the poem, five pages long, is rich in imagery and metaphors, elaborated across line after line, often interrupted by parentheses and intercalated subclauses. The effect is of striking lines buried in a cascade of words; intermittently exact and singingly sharp ('So in late evening, the elegy/ of day asserts itself; and knowing/ we are breathing we make the most of breath'), yet crowded out by language that prefers to encircle its subject than directly to take hold of it. But this early poem looks twenty five years ahead to one of Ormond's most characteristic and achieved later works, 'Definition of a Waterfall':

Not stitched to air or water but to both
A veil hangs broken in concealing truth

And flies in vague exactitude, a dove
Born diving between rivers out of love

'Definition of a Waterfall' is a tight, compressed poem that uses paradox to clarify rather than befuddle:

From ledge to pool breakneck across rocks
Wild calm, calm chaos skein their paradox

So that excited poise is fiercely dressed
In a long instant's constant flow of rest,

So that this bridegroom and his bride in white
Parting together headlong reunite

Among her trailing braids. The inconstancy
Is reconciled to fall, falls and falls free

There is, first, the unobtrusive but binding alliteration which, coupled with the rich end-rhymes that contrast with, and momentarily stall, the overrunning syntax of the lines, allows the poem's movement to enact something of the paradox of fixity-in-flow that it describes. Yet for all this ingenuity of structuring, the sense stays clear, and as the central conceit emerges – the bride and groom 'parting together' – it resolves itself into something visually immediate, satisfying to the ear, and intellectually persuasive. The poem begins with a negative, 'Not', which it quickly redeems into a double positive: 'Not [..] but [...] both'. This is the beauty of paradox, that (when it succeeds) it holds aloft a contradiction in such a way as to enhance rather than to deplete the proposition. We can see why this is one of Ormond's anthology pieces: memorable, precisely crafted, intricate without being showy, it speaks of what passes and what goes, of movement and stasis, of Time and love, freedom and constraint. The poem has an exuberance about it, an inventive daring, that belies the careful way in which its components dovetail into each other; how, to borrow a fittingly elegant term from carpentry, they *marry*. Yet it has something of the early Ormond to it too, and indeed a version of it may well date from 1947. Like 'Birthday Poem', it is a poem about love, perhaps even a love poem. But the *élan* has been tamed, the love of paradox disciplined, the surprising imagery made to work as part of a whole rather than as an explosive but short-lived assault on the line. Wynn Thomas, in his book on Ormond, describes Ormond's technique here and in a number of other later poems:

silhouetting the otherwise ungraspable essence of a phenomenon by outlining it with conceits (rather as a knife-thrower carves out the shape of a living target which remains untouched).

The analogy with the knife-thrower is an inspired one, and perfect in the way it rephrases Mallarmé's famous definition of the poet's task: 'to evoke, through a precise shadow, the unspoken object'.

Until *Requiem* and *Celebration*, which appeared in 1969, Ormond's poems had only appeared in magazines and anthologies. This partly accounts for the sense we have of his being a sort of long-established newcomer to the poetry 'scene'. Composed as it is of work from nearly three decades, *Requiem* and *Celebration* seemed written by at least two different poets. This is often the way with first collections, thought first collections rarely appear when their author is forty-six. Ormond was by then a distinguished documentary filmmaker in Cardiff, where he moved in 1955, after leaving London and *Picture Post*, and after a five-year stint as a sub-editor with the *South Wales Evening Post*. By the end of the 1960s, Ormond had a substantial body of television and radio work behind him, including films about Dylan Thomas, Vernon Watkins, Richard Burton, Ceri Richards, Robert Graves and Alun Lewis. Though he had been publishing regularly in the literary press in Wales and beyond – poems, reviews, but also critical articles and journalism on literature and the visual arts – Ormond had yet to gather together a unified collection. To put this into context, let us recall what his contemporaries had already published: Dannie Abse, his friend and a valuable critic of his work, had published seven volumes, including a *Selected* in 1963; R.S. Thomas ten; Roland Mathias four. In British poetry more generally, the 1940s in which Ormond began were now a forgotten decade, a sprawling intermission between the generation of Auden and The Movement. Larkin, Gunn, Davie, Amis, Ted Hughes had all brought out notable collections, while anthologies such as Alvarez's *The New Poetry* (1962) had helped introduce the work of Lowell, Berryman, Plath and others to Britain.

While it may be said that media work had taken time from Ormond's poetry, especially given his prolific documentary output, it is likely that it also brought something to it. We may leave scholars to speculate about how, precisely, filmmaking may have contributed to Ormond's poetic style over the 1960s. However, there is one way in which it directly caused poetry to happen. In 1963, making a documentary in Arezzo, *From a Town in Tuscany*, Ormond recalled hearing workmen whistling as they worked on the church of Santa Maria della Pieve. When the poem came two years later, Ormond recalls it making itself 'in 50 minutes flat ... it just seemed to come down my arm without my thought, and it broke the blockage that had kept me virtually silent for so many years. It was like nothing I had ever written before.' The poem was 'Cathedral Builders'.

'Cathedral Builders' is a homage to craft and skill, but also to the ordinariness of the artist – and to the possibility, always humbling and frequently useful to bear in mind, that artistry is not the sole privilege of the 'artist'. The poem imagines the lives of craftsmen, and salvages their individuality and their voices – which, tellingly, end the poem. There is something in this poem that makes us think of Ruskin's great treatise, 'The Nature of Gothic', in which he lauds Gothic architecture not just for its beauty but for its imperfection, and specifically – Ruskin's art criticism being a passionate advocacy of the dignity of labour – for the way it allows the craftsmen, however poor, anonymous and downtrodden they may have been, to express themselves spiritually through their manual skill. For Ruskin, it is the imperfection of Gothic that makes it human and organic, that enables it to stand against both the abstraction and regularity of the classical, to which he opposed it as architecture, and to resist the mechanisation and enslavement of labour he saw in capitalist society. What Ruskin called the 'moral and imaginative elements' of Gothic are thus as much social as they are aesthetic. The architect, he writes

must take his workmen as he finds them, and let them show their weaknesses together with their strength, which will involve the Gothic imperfection, but render the whole work as noble as the intellect of the age can make it.

Ormond's poem, while certainly grounded in his own understanding of and respect for the industrial history of his own country, invests equally deeply in the idea of work as an expression of the total human being. Here too he plays with paradox, what we might call the intimate distance between the artwork and its maker:

They climbed on sketchy ladders towards God,
With winch and pulley hoisted hewn rock into heaven,
Inhabited the sky with hammers, defied gravity,
Deified stone, took up God's house to meet him,

And came down to their suppers and small beer,
Every night slept, lay with their smelly wives,
Quarrelled and cuffed the children,
Lied, spat, sang, were happy, or unhappy...

The cathedral builders are given back their ordinariness, even as the cathedral they erect climbs skywards (they 'Saw naves sprout arches, clerestories soar'). They watch their work being finished off by others, engaged in a collective enterprise of individual expressions. The poem plays on the vertical axis too, playing off the humdrum, grounded lives of the builders against the spiritual ascent of worship. As well as verticality, 'Cathedral Builders' works in counterpoint: the beauty of the cathedral against the gritty, grimy reality it climbs free of yet owes its making to. Ormond's poem demystifies art but elevates it too, and does so with humour. By the end, the builders decide 'to leave the spire to others'; at the cathedral's consecration, they 'Stood in the crowd' [...], Envied the fat bishop his warm boots,/ Cocked up a squint eye, and said, 'I bloody did that'".

Whether we read this ending as a statement of craftsmanly pride, class resentment or both at once, it is significant that Ormond ends the poem with that ambiguous last line, bringing the whole skyscraping edifice back down to earth, but without bathos. The poem is not just about cathedrals, workers, social class and the gap between spiritual matters and everyday life. The cathedral is like the poem, and like all works of art: it is a made thing that outlasts both its making and its maker. In this sense, the phrase 'I bloody did that' has a further dimension: it is the cry of the maker, prideful but also ambivalent, who realises that his work is at once the fullest expression of himself and something he no longer owns; that, like the cathedral builders, he stands as an onlooker to the consecration – through reading, which is the poem's consecration – of an object that was, but is no longer, his.

The reason this poem seems representative of Ormond is that it joins together several of his preoccupations as a mature poet: an interest in craft and in truth to materials, in the social context of art, but also its time- and place-transcendent value. It is far from being a religious poem, and as we have seen it deftly plays off the spirit's ascent against the body's downward pull, but it chooses a demotic and accessible way of expressing the chasm between the two. In fact, it values that chasm, sees it as part of art's premise, and part of great art's understanding of its condition. It is no coincidence that Ormond's W.D. Thomas memorial lecture in Swansea in 1983 took as its title Wallace Stevens's line from 'Blue Guitar: 'Poetry/ Exceeding music must take the place/ Of empty heaven and its hymns'. 'In Place of Empty Heaven', Ormond called the lecture, and Stevens, in many ways the heir to Mallarmé and the French Symbolists, was clearly a reference-point for him, as for so many other poets preoccupied with the status of art as a truthful fiction. It is what Mallarmé called the 'Glorious Lie' we set against the 'Nothingness we know to be the truth'. Wallace Stevens rephrases this for a different moment and a different poetic tradition when he writes in *Adagia*: 'The final belief is to believe in a fiction, which you know to be a fiction, there being nothing else. The exquisite truth is to know that it is a fiction and that you believe in it willingly.'

II

John Ormond was born in 1923, in Dunvant near Swansea, in the same community as the painter Ceri Richards, to whom Ormond wrote an elegy ('Salmon': 'first for, and now in memory of, Ceri Richards') and about whom he made a film in 1967. His father was a shoemaker and many of his relatives worked in the coal mines. Several of the poems in *Requiem* and *Celebration*, notably 'My Dusty Kinsfolk' and 'At his Father's Grave', written in the early 1950s, are about the people and places of his youth. Elegiac in tenor, these poems are, in their spare and often understated way, homages to a living past; indeed the title 'Requiem and Celebration' does not refer to two ways of remembering but to a single, mingled, one. Ormond recalls that Welsh and English 'existed side by side' in Dunvant, though there was little Welsh in his home and he himself was not a natural Welsh-speaker. Educated at Swansea Grammar School and then at Swansea University, Ormond studied philosophy under the Wittgenstein scholar Rush Rhees, graduating in philosophy in 1944, and in English in 1945. It was through Rhees that Ormond met Wittgenstein, and it is interesting to speculate about how contact with Wittgenstein's ideas on the philosophy side of Ormond's intellectual formation might have combined with the prevailing sweep of the poetry he would have been immersed in at the time. After all, the philosopher of lapidary terseness sits ill with the lyric exorbitance of Dylan Thomas and his circle. Nonetheless, we might argue that for Ormond's purposes a scepticism about language is a prerequiste for using it well; the fact that his early poems do not necessarily reflect this does not mean that the ideas that would later temper their extravagance and imitativeness were not there. And besides, there is no better prompt to using language frugally than the realisation that one has spent too long spending it to excess.

By the time he left university, Ormond had already published poems in magazines and been anthologised. In 1943, he appeared – still as John Ormond Thomas – in the book *Indications*, along with James Kirkup and John Bayliss, published by the London publisher Grey Walls Press, founded by Charles Wrey Gardiner, editor of *Poetry Quarterly*. The press and the magazine (where Ormond also published) were notable conduits for the New Romantic and Apocalypse poets, and one of the poets associated with them, to whom Ormond dedicated 'Poem at the Beginning of Winter', was Alex Comfort, who edited several of the Grey Walls anthologies.

Ormond was a conscientious objector, not uncommon among Welsh poets in both languages. For this, he appeared before a tribunal and incurred the disapprobation of his English professor, W.D. Thomas (whose memorial lecture on Stevens he would later give). Like Dylan Thomas, Vernon Watkins, Keidrych Rhys and Lynette Roberts, Ormond wrote poetry that spoke of the horrors of war from the point of view of its effects on civilian populations, notably the bombing raids on industrial cities such as Swansea, which was badly damaged by aerial attack from the Luftwaffe. Among the most achieved of the early poems is 'Funeral of a German Airman', which appeared in *Poetry Folios 5* in 1944. Ormond uses the poem to denationalise conflict, and chooses to commemorate the airman as a representative of all combatants. This is among those early poems that stand out for their clarity of conception and the relative spareness of their diction. Swansea had suffered its last devastating attack on February 16 1943, and a German plane had been shot down. The body of Obergefreiter Kurt Brand, the flight's observer, was washed up in April on Rhossili beach and his funeral held in Killay, close to Dunvant. Ormond imagines the body 'searching the seas blindly for a grave' before finding land on 'an enemy but a friendly shore'. It is, to say the least, an unusual perspective for a poet to take in the heat of war:

> Though smothered under your flag, as all soldiers
> are smothered, limbs irresistibly tied
> By the knots of no-cause and all-too-certain death,
> I say your heart is still in flower
> shedding this futile badge, as futile as our crosses.

The pacifism is clear, as is the anti-nationalism, something that would emerge, albeit unobtrusively, in Ormond's own refusal to become drawn into the various nationalisms, both Welsh and British, on offer in the Wales of the 1960s and 70s. The soldier is, like all soldiers, 'smothered' by a national flag; the military decorations, like the cross, mean nothing and bring no comfort to a man 'who perhaps at the point of a gun/ had a gun placed in his hand'. Ormond's finest poems of this period are those that take war as their subject or their impetus. 'City in Fire and Snow' is an elaborate and over-long, but in parts controlled, poem about the devastating three-day aerial bombing of Swansea on 19, 20 and 21 February 1941. Though Ormond did not begin the poem until 1948 (he finished it in 1952), it is a powerful dream-like narrative which owes too much to Vernon Watkins and specifically to Dylan Thomas's 'Refusal to Mourn' to be entirely Ormond's own work. More achieved is the 1944 'Selections from an Elegy for Alun Lewis', which appeared in that year's June issue of Keidrych Rhys's *Wales*.

> Poets are few, and those who fall
> into the unmeasured, almost
> unpremeditated darkness
> forestall their vision, as fliers
> at night seeking the unblemished north
> with instruments not perfectly adjusted.

It is a tender and moving poem (it appeared alongside other elegies for Lewis by Brenda Chamberlain and Vernon Watkins), and that likening of poet to pilot, of poetic vision to night vision, is strikingly well-found. The 'unmeasured, almost/ unpremeditated darkness' is a finely hesitant line, and that 'almost', which might in another poet's hands be merely vaguening, carries a weight of thought, slows down the line and attenuates the grandeur of the statement: the poet as an Icarus of the night sky, his 'instruments not perfectly adjusted' (a very Audenesque line). Poetry, suggests Ormond, is also a matter of 'instruments', of 'adjustment', of technique and precision. Ormond expands, and perhaps over-expands, the metaphor, by referring, in the next stanza, to the pilot's log, to the scrambled code, and to the untaken path of the downed airman-poet. These are close enough to clichés, and perhaps that is what they are in the abstract: poetry as a private language, the poet as 'Seer' or visionary, the body of youthful work felled in its prime and leaving ghost *oeuvre* haunting the future. But the metaphor holds and stays in our mind, both because it is concisely handled and because it comes from the lived reality of war.

There is something opportunistic about reading a poet's early experiments for signs of the later work, not least because it leads us to find only what we were looking for. To say that there is enough in Ormond's first period to catch sight of the sort of poet he would later become is not to dismiss the rest, but to acknowledge how immersed he was in the poetic culture that surrounded him, both in a Welsh context and in the wider British one. To the more durable poems of or about the 1940s, we might add the 'Portraits' of his grandfather, father and mother, and the poems on the births of his children, as poems that stand out from what is essentially a skilled apprenticeship, not just in poetry but in influence and how to manage it.

Work – first as a staff writer for *Picture Post* in London, then as a sub-editor for the *Swansea Evening Post*, and finally as a filmmaker for BBC Wales – meant that Ormond devoted less time to poetry. But having a job undoubtedly enlarged his sense of poetry's place and context. By this is not simply meant its connectedness to the other arts – especially, in Ormond's case, the visual arts – but its place in a world where other things happen. This is rare among poets, who tend to treasure their marginality as the next best thing to their imagined centrality (some even prefer it). One of the most rewarding exercises for Ormond was writing poems in response to photographs in the *News Chronicle* during the mid-1950s. Ormond's 'Saturday Picture' verses are far removed from the learned ekphrastic sallies we often find when poets write from or around images. They are immediate and accessible, often witty and affectionate, their lyricism delicate, and they have a humorous social realism to them. Here is 'Mirror', which appeared in September 1956:

> A peeling mirror at an auction sale
> A gazing girl, together tell a tale
> That springs from more than casual connection:
> It is the imperfection of reflection.
> All glass is false. What image does not twist
> Beauty the wrong way round? So truth is missed.
> Yet Beauty, bidding against Isolation,
> Will take the second-best, approximation.

However prompted by images these poems might once have been, they clearly no longer depend upon them. What strikes us is how much intelligence and lyric craft Ormond brings to these 'occasional' poems – 'occasional' only in the sense that, like all good poems, they climb free of what occasioned them. This edition contains enough of these 'Saturday Pictures' to show what a valuable addition to his work they are, not just for their economy of means, but for their ability to balance a sense of a wider readership with the depth and compression of their ideas. There may be an adjustment of the 'instruments' of verse, but there is never any suggestion of 'talking down' to readers. The sense that poetry might be successfully woven into ordinary reading practices as well as daily life without hazarding its status as art is certainly something that Ormond holds to, and it informs his creative work across a range of media.

Ormond is a skilful narrator, and a humorous one too. In 'The Birth of Venus at Aberystwyth', he takes the trope of Venus born from the sea (Rimbaud's 'Vénus Anadyomène' is its most glorious debunking) and transposes it to sleepy seaside Wales:

> Beyond the pier varicose waves crocheted
> A complex permanent nothing on the stones.
> The Corporation deck-chairs flapped
> Haphazard unison. Most sea-front windows
>
> Confessed to Vacancies; and on the promenade
> A violinist in Scotch-plaid dinner-jacket
> Contributed little to the Welsh way of life
> As he played 'Thanks for the Memory'

To two small children and a dog.

There is something Larkinesque about this anti-heroic poem as it fugues amusingly on middlebrow bleakness. The 'complex permanent nothing' belongs to a different register from what follows it, but it gains from the juxtaposition too: the 'varicose waves' which both suggest the shape and colour of the waves and, more deflatingly, the ageing if not already agèd population of the town. The reader who knows their Anglo-Welsh poetry might see an additional affinity here with John Tripp, whose *Selected Poems* Ormond edited in 1987, a pungent if limited poet whose stock-in-trade was railing against the depredations wreaked by colonisation, modernity, anglicisation and geriatricisation (if the word exists) upon Welsh life. When this sort of thing works, it works well, but not often, and Ormond has the judgment to do it properly once and once only. It gives an idea of Ormond's range, however, and shows us how he could turn to a variety of styles to suit particular moods and moments. To say that there is what might be called an 'Ormond poem' – we think, for instance of 'Definition of a Waterfall', 'The Gift', 'Cathedral Builders', 'Finding a Fossil', 'Salmon' or 'Tuscan Cypresses' – does not mean there were not plenty of other styles he could turn his hand to.

Like Abse, like Tripp, like R.S. Thomas, Alun Lewis, Lynette Roberts and other Anglo-Welsh poets, he engaged with the Welsh-language tradition, but from a distance. 'Lament for a Leg', for instance, is written in the voice of Henry Hughes, a cooper, whose leg and thigh are buried near the famous yew tree in Cardiganshire where Dafydd ap Gwilym rests. As the poem's epigraph reads, 'the rest of Henry Hughes set off across the Atlantic in search of better fortune'. The usual pieties by which one invokes one's predecessors are not to be found in Ormond's poem, but it remains, in its way, a tribute: first, to the world's also-rans, the 'buried-alongsides', the accidental passengers in the slipstream of history; and second, to Dafydd ap Gwilym himself, to the mix of intricacy, craft, wisdom and sheer ribaldry that the medieval poet so joyously combined. Ormond's Henry Hughes ends the poem with his own *risqué* joke, his allusion to Dafydd's 'Penis' poem ('Y Gal' in the Welsh):

What will the great God say
At Dafydd's wild-kicking-climbing extra leg,

Jammed hard in heaven's white doorway
(I'll limp unnimble round the narrow back)
Come the quick trumpet of the Judgement Day?

'Design for a Quilt' is another poem that combines the high and the low. With its tight sound-patterning, its subtle syntactical inversions and that oddly archaic dynamism of phrasing one enjoys in great translations of old poems, it has the feel of translatedness without sounding like translationese. It is a very difficult thing to bring off. It is as if Ormond were transposing himself to one of Dafydd's coterie of bards in an act of poetic ventriloquism:

First let there be a tree, roots taking ground
In bleached and soft blue fabric.
Into the well-aired sky branches extend
Only to bend away from the turned-back
Edge of linen where day's horizons end;

Branches symmetrical, not over-flaunting
Their leaves (let ordinary swansdown
Be their lining), which in the summertime
Will lie lightly upon her, the girl
This quilt's for, this object of designing;

As the poem ends, we see that this beautiful and complex design, like the poem that describes it and enumerates its features, has an altogether earthier agenda:

So that in future times, recalling
The pleasures of past falling, she'll bequeath it
To one or other of the line,
Bearing her name or mine,
With luck I'll help her make beneath it.

This is less the eroticised wit of the metaphysicals such as Donne or Marvell than the salty ribaldry of the medieval court poets, or of the Troubadours. There is an erotic strain to Ormond's poetry, perhaps best exemplified in the long poem 'Salmon':

The stream slides clear yet shirred

With broken surfaces where
Stones trap the creamy stars

Of air, she scoops at gravel with fine
Thrust of her exact blind tail;
   At last her lust
Gapes in a gush on her stone nest
And his held, squanderous peak
Shudders his final hunger
On her milk; seed laid on seed
In spunk of liquid silk.
So in exhausted saraband their slack
Convulsions wind and wend galactic
   Seed in seed, a found
   World without end.

The poem is a homage to Richards that became, between first and second publications (first in *Poetry Wales* and then, after Richards death in 1971, in *Definition of a Waterfall* in 1973) become a sort of elegy. What strikes us about this poem is the way it revisits not just Ormond's own earliest style, but perhaps, in revisiting it, celebrates the whole period in which he was formed as a poet: the world of Dylan Thomas and Vernon Watkins, Ceri Richards and Graham Sutherland, and the poetry of the 1940s more generally, with its hunger for words and images and its insistence on the unconscious life-force. 'Salmon' takes up once more the energy and organicism of the early poems, but does so in a structured rush, in order to speak of life, death and rebirth. There are ways of reckoning, poetically, with one's younger self without disowning it, and this seems to me to be Ormond's living epitaph for a time, a style and a self, that, like the salmon, have died in order to be reborn. In his elegy for Robert Duncan, 'Duncan', Thom Gunn says something important about how poets negotiate their beginnings: 'He learned/ You add to, you don't cancel what you do'. Whatever Ormond may have cancelled about his 1940s, 'Salmon' plunges back into them while adding something new.

To contrast with 'Salmon', but still embedded in nature, we might compare 'Finding a Fossil', which seems to still the dynamism of the natural world, to freeze it as a still might freeze a moment in a filmic sequence:

Maidenhair fern in flint;
An ancient accident
Shows me time's imprint.

A leaf preserved and pressed
Between leaves of stone; crossed
Rest and unrest.

Movement caught in stillness, life captured in lifelessness, the impermanent becoming permanent... all these themes preoccupy Ormond across the range of his poetries: 'remembered shapes/ Live', he writes, and 'Love speaks as loves lapse'. What dies dies into a different kind of life, and there is a bleakness to the statement 'Love speaks as loves lapse' – as if words are found only when the emotions that drive them into becoming have gone. The poem's tight rhyming, its short, direct statements, have the kind of expansiveness of meaning that is achieved only through mastering compression. As for the 'leaves' of the plant and the 'leaves' of the stone, these might also be the leaves of a book, the pages on which the poem is printed and imprinted.

'Illuminations on the Letter O' is among those poems that bear the obvious trace of poets such as Wallace Stevens. The poem cleverly ghost-rhymes the sound of the letter O with words, such as 'snow' and 'zero' that evoke the paradox of something being nothing, nothing being something: the perfect circle and the perfect cycle. The scribe who decorates the illuminated manuscript is also tracing his mark on the emptiness of the margins, leaving his prints on the 'parish of snow'. Fugueing on whiteness, blankness, emptiness, but also on writing, on filling the page, on conquering the void, Ormond is exploring the making of art. It is obviously significant that Ormond chooses a religious subject but does not explore it religiously, preferring instead the richer territory of what Mallarmé called the 'blank abyss' for which the page stands:

Brocade and embellishment
At the round boundary, a garland,
A gold-leaf beating of bounds
About the parish of snow:

Transfixed in wading the white acres,

Jailed in his pretty prison,
The subject of the text he cannot walk in   .
Is the sole occupant of zero;

There is a continuity of preoccupation here with a poem such as
'Cathedral Builders', at first sight so different in tone and manner: it
is the question of the maker's relationship with the made, and with
the ways in which we fill our emptiness with art. Whiteness stands of
course for purity, but also for sterility, for what is invisible but there.
A challenge to the poet in its manifestation on the unwritten page,
blankness continues to hold sway in the margins of the poem, the
place where words do not reach, but where the mind slides. In one of
the 'Saturday Picture' poems, 'Gulls', Ormond describes the un-
neutral neutrality of white:

The war of flight. Neutrality's restraint
From early sunlight mustering new brightness.
Instant of new possession, new complaint.
Instant of whiteness overtaking whiteness.

This short poem contains no colours; instead it enumerates the
whiteness of the wings, the whiteness of the spume that rides the
waves, and the whiteness of the snow. By rights, this scene should be
invisible, and perhaps it is, but the poem's verbs of action – 'startled
and startling whiteness' – ensure that language draws out its drama,
its dynamism. The poem may certainly be indebted to Vernon
Watkins's 'Music of Colours', which opens 'O, but how white is
white, white form shadows come/ Sailing white of clouds, not seen
before/ On any snowfield, any shore'. Equally pertinent comparisons
would be Gautier's 'Symphony in White Major' and Mallarmé's 'The
Virginal, the Lively and the Beautiful Today', both of which are
'about' swans, though only in the way *Moby Dick* is 'about' a whale.
Gautier's poem (Watkins had translated several Gautier poems) is
sensual and erotic, his 'swan-women' imagined with their
'debaucheries of whiteness', while Mallarmé's poem is more implic-
itly about writing, as it describes a swan frozen in the ice and unable
to rise and fly, its plumage (the French for fountain pen is 'plume',
or feather) caught in the ice. Ormond's own symphony in white is
more quotidian – seagulls tangling in the wind – but in its way
equally metaphysical, with 'whiteness overtaking whiteness' to create

a scene that is vibrant with danger and life.

Ormond is attuned to the way in which absence and presence are, in poetry at least, less opposites than productively conflicting ingredients – the material for paradox, in fact. In a fine late poem, 'Blue Bath-Gown', published in 1989, the year before his death, he takes the mundane touch of his wife's gown and builds from it not just a love-poem but a poem about the way the heart and mind work with absence to conjure up, in a sort of hologram, a fullness and a presence. Memory re-makes the lost intensities of life and perhaps perfects them, just as the fossil perfects, in making permanent, the fern whose imprint it takes. This way of working with the negative, with what is not there, in order to redeem it into meaning and existence, is something we see across his work. 'Blue Bath Gown' is an example as much of his sensibility, his way of thinking, as it is of his ease in managing often abstract concepts:

How things summon up their opposites:
Heat cold, togetherness apart,
The staircase up the same staircase
Down; dawn dusk, sunlight and snow
In the one heart.

There's no dividing them.

Ormond is not a difficult poet, if by 'difficult' we mean that he draws on allusions which, unknown to the reader, impede the poem's reception. But he is an intellectually stringent one. A great deal has been made of the craftedness of his verse, of the precision of his diction and of the way in which he handles concepts that in other hands might become abstractions. But more than this, his best poems do more than put words to ideas; they give body to thought.

Patrick McGuinness 2015

Acknowledgments

It's a pleasure to record a debt to John Ormond's best critics, Wynn Thomas and Richard Poole. Their work, always enlightening, has been invaluable to me here.

I would like to thank Charles Mundye and Angharad Price for help with this introduction, and to pay a happy debt to Cary Archard, who first suggested I read John Ormond and who introduced me to Ormond's widow, Glenys, soon after I came to live in Cardiff.

Most of all, I'm grateful to Rian Evans, John Ormond's daughter, who reads her father's work with the same qualities he brought to writing it: love matched by rigour.

P McG

An Ormond Chronology

1923

Ormond was born John Ormond Thomas on 3 April in Bridge Terrace, Dunvant, to Elsie and Arthur Thomas, village shoemaker. They were not a nuclear family: Elsie's father (the grandfather of the apple-tree) lived with them, as did her brother Emlyn. Ormond's only child status was mitigated by the friendship of his first cousins of whom there were many, since his mother was the youngest of 10. Closest in his affections were Edna, Leslie, Eileen and Granville, the children of Elsie's sister Mary, married to Willie Beynon. Their house on Dunvant's other hill, just above Ebenezer chapel, would spell a sort of salvation. Ebenezer itself was the hub of the village community, its cultural life rich even by Welsh standards: choral singing, oratorio performances, theatrical productions and discussion groups were all part of the normal calendar. The painter Ceri Richards, born in Dunvant in 1903, recognised the importance of this vibrant background, in particular the music, to his artistic development. Similarly, Granville Beynon, who became an eminent physicist, knighted for his contribution to science, always paid tribute to the part that Dunvant's ferment of activity had played in shaping his life.

1928

A somewhat sickly child — he had rheumatic fever twice, one bout confining him to bed for a whole year — Ormond missed a good deal of early schooling at Dunvant's Primary School. But he was curious and sensitive, and being read to by anyone who could spare the time helped instil a passion for books. Though his grandfather and his mother's eldest siblings were all Welsh-speaking, the youngest were not; so while Ormond heard Welsh spoken around the village, with chapel services always bilingual, English was the language of home and of learning.

1935

Ormond went to Swansea Grammar School, *Virtue and Good Literature* the school motto. The railway bridge just yards from their house marked the boundary of the schools catchment area so, rather than Gowerton Grammar School where most of the rest of the village went, Ormond, here again something of a loner, went in to Swansea. In the upper school, he went on to be taught by senior English master, D.J. Thomas, father of Dylan. The latter had been a pupil there, but, being eight and a half years older, had already left when Ormond was just beginning.

1939

At Higher, he studied English, French and History; his preferred subjects of Art, Physics and Maths were not deemed a viable combination, putting paid to hopes of a career in art or architecture. Surprisingly, given the childhood history of illness, he was a strong rugby wing and a talented athlete, victor ludorum in June's school sports and due to run for Wales but denied that with the advent of the war. Ormond was already a committed pacifist: from his early teenage years he had attended Peace Pledge Union meetings with his cousin Granville, nine years his senior and something of a mentor. But war soon enough came horribly close to home.

1941

18th February 1941 is the date on Ormond's copy of Baudelaire's *Les Fleurs du Mal*. It proved symbolic. The German Luftwaffe blitzed Swansea from the 19th to the 21st of February and Swansea Grammar School was badly bombed, along with much of the town. Encountering poems by Wilfred Owen and Dylan Thomas, just weeks after the German blitz, hit him with a parallel emotional force. That spring effectively determined his future. Ormond became an avid collector of books, mainly bought cheaply at Ralph's Secondhand Bookshop in Swansea, and the unusual range of his reading is an indication of his tastes and ambitions. His schoolfriend, Bill Price, attests to his always going well beyond the requirements of the syllabus and to his reading aloud poems which fired his imagination. He had already acquired the habit of visiting the nearby Glynn Vivian Gallery of a lunchtime. Later that year, Ormond went on to University College, Swansea, where he read Philosophy and English. He maintained his interest in art by going to life-drawing classes at Swansea Art College in tandem with, occasionally instead of, his university classes. The iconic Catholic imagery in many of his early poems – entirely at odds with Ebenezer's strict non-conformism – seems to relate to the pictures by Renaissance painters he sought out at the art school library. Decades later, after visiting Italy and Spain for the first time, he would return to similar images and themes. At college, Ormond was the only philosophy student not preparing for the ministry; the others were by and large Welsh-speaking, among them poets writing in Welsh. He bought what they published and apparently also studied the strict metrical rules of *cynghanedd* with interest.

1942

Ormond's poems were accepted for publication outside Wales, the first in the autumn edition of *Poetry Quarterly* and, by 1943, his work was appearing not only in the slim volume, *Indications*, together with that of John Bayliss and James Kirkup, but in other magazines and anthologies as well. It is surely no coincidence that many of the poets and writers with whom he was being published were pacifists. At college, Ormond had already appeared before a conscientious objectors' tribunal, incurring the wrath of his professor of English, W.D. Thomas, commander of the college's R.A.F. cadet unit. Others were more sympathetic to his stance, and he later cited two lecturers as important to his intellectual development: the first was the English Department's Thomas Taig who, in due course, would introduce him to the poet Vernon Watkins, home on leave from the R.A.F.; the second was his philosophy lecturer, the American Rush Rhees, whose critical approach to ideas and the world certainly influenced Ormond's thinking. It was through Rhees that he met Ludwig Wittgenstein and, though professing never to have liked him, was apparently happy enough to argue with him about concepts of time. Swansea was the place to which students of University College, London, were evacuated and the mix was enriching, but it was a local boy who became another life-long friend. Wynn Williams was from Briton Ferry, reading geography and geology, passionate about music – they often sang as a duo – and about poetry. It was at college too that Ormond fell in love with Glenys Roderick, his junior by just a year and taking a degree in Welsh and English. The professor of education, Fred Schonell, best known for his pioneering work on children's reading, admired her quick mind; she was captain of the college hockey and tennis teams, but perhaps best testimony to her particular strength of character was her decision to study German during these war years. She was deeply sympathetic to Ormond's pacifist beliefs, coming as she did from Loughor, whose young men had been decimated during the Great War.

1945

Ormond graduated with an honours degree in English, having gained a final degree in Philosophy the previous year. On leaving college, he briefly became a reporter at the *Brentwood Gazette*, almost immediately required to work out his notice on being offered a trial period at *Picture Post*, the most celebrated magazine of its day. He had written to the editor, Tom Hopkinson, and was invited for interview on the strength of the poems he had submitted. After three months, he was made a staff writer, still only 22. His colleagues included Sydney (later Lord) Jacobson, Lionel (Bobby) Birch, Ted Castle (husband of the Labour politician, Barbara Castle), Fyfe Robertson, later of Tonight fame, and Bert Lloyd who, as well as being a journalist, was both a practitioner and authority on folk-singing. Working alongside some of the finest photographers and following the Hopkinson maxim of using words sparingly to ensure primacy of the image, this period would establish the pattern of Ormond's future working methods. At the time, it was remarkable for the variety and scope of the weekly briefs he was given: among others, he would meet and write about the tenor Beniamino Gigli, the Inkspots and Bernard Shaw, and his portrait of Blaenau Ffestiniog's slate-mine included, in translation, a poem by one of the miners, by way of underlining the legacy across the social spectrum of Wales's ancient literary traditions. He clearly thrived on the challenges. Yet his letters suggest pangs of *hiraeth* for home and for Glenys, by now teaching at Cardigan Grammar School, but it's safe to assume there was some consolation in the pubs of Fleet Street and those of Soho which, as in the war years, were still the meeting-places of writers and artists.

1946

Picture Post staff were also responsible in their turn for seeing the magazine through the press each week: from this stemmed Ormond's abiding love for the whole business of print and printing. In June, *Picture Post* also provided him with his first opportunity to meet and profile Dylan Thomas who was living in Oxford at the time. While there had earlier been a brief exchange of letters, they had not met and the frequently-quoted description of the young Ormond "sitting at the feet of Dylan and Vernon" is accurate only in the metaphorical sense. In September, Ormond and Glenys were married, moving to a flat in Datchet which they took over from Granville Beynon, who until then had been working at the National Physics Laboratory in Slough. Glenys taught in Slough before the birth of their daughter Eirianedd (Rian) in October 1947.

1948

At the end of the summer, Ormond's most unusual *Picture Post* assignment took him with photographer Hayward Magee to the South of France to cover the return of W.B. Yeats's body to Ireland. It was his carefully-worded article of the 9th of October that first suggested a confusion over bodies, namely that the body shipped back for re-burial with state ceremony in Drumcliffe in County Sligo, was not actually the body of W.B. Yeats. Ormond was bitterly disappointed that such an extraordinary story was not followed through at the time – a diplomatic veil drawn over it – nor indeed when he tried to write it at greater length in retirement. It would be more than sixty years before it emerged again, thanks to the revelations of Louise Foxcroft, the great-niece of Alfred Hollis who, like Yeats, had died on 28 January 1939 and whose body was mistakenly taken to be that of Yeats. Despite the pressure of work at Shoe Lane, Ormond continued to have poems published and also broadcast on radio by the BBC.

1949

Ormond's decision to return to Swansea, working at the *South Wales Evening Post* as a sub-editor, was hasty and taken for different reasons, some of which he later regretted. He soon came to find the duties mundane and, though he also worked as a stringer for *Time-Life* magazine, his hope of having more time for his own writing wasn't entirely fulfilled. But, with the *Post* job, came a rented house and, during these early years of the new decade, it would be an idyllic home for his growing family.

1950

His son Huw Garan was born in April but, by December of the same year, his father Arthur had died of cancer. The poem 'My Dusty Kinsfolk' set in the graveyard of Ebenezer, was written following his father's death and its final line "I speak these words to you, my kin/ And friends, in requiem and celebration" is almost a defining perception of his future role as a poet. Compensation for any disillusion in the early 50s would come in the bonds of friendship forged with Daniel Jones, Vernon Watkins, Fred Janes and Alban Leyshon, Charles Fisher and other members of Dylan Thomas's Kardomah gang, though Thomas himself was less frequently in Swansea at this time. Their mix of intellect and rapier wit was hugely stimulating and perhaps the greatest compliment they could have paid the relative youngster and Johnny-come-lately was accepting him as one of the gang. They would remain close long after Thomas's death.

1952
Hugh Cudlipp offered Ormond a job as a columnist on *The Daily Mirror* but he declined it; returning to London by now held less attraction. While he still found subbing a drudgery, the *Evening Post* offered opportunities for book-reviewing, which he enjoyed. When Ormond's review of Dylan Thomas's *Collected Poems* – "one of the literary events of the century" he had concluded – was published on the 8th of November, Thomas had apparently been outside the building where he himself had worked as a reporter, waiting for the first edition to come off the press. Thomas, having read Ormond's observation that the influence of Thomas Traherne was to be found in his writing, later remarked to him that it was quite true, but that no-one had picked up on it before. The ensuing discussion seems to have marked the beginning of closer friendship. Ormond's radio play, *Man in Darkness*, a mystery play and allegory with music specially composed by Daniel Jones, was broadcast in the BBC Welsh Region on December 15.

1953
Dylan Thomas's death in New York in November came as a massive blow. Ormond helped Daniel Jones, Dylan's closest friend, in making the funeral arrangements and they went together to Southampton to meet the ship bearing Thomas's body. Back in Laugharne they sat with Florence Thomas, Dylan's mother, as she contemplated the open coffin in her parlour. Dr. Jones's account of this in the opening page of his memoir *My Friend Dylan Thomas* goes some way to explaining what for Ormond became a tortured memory, perpetuated for him by the bronze death-mask of Dylan made by sculptor David Slivka.

1954
In January, Thomas's *Under Milk Wood* was broadcast on BBC radio and Ormond was a member of the cast, albeit a lowly one, playing Cherry Owen and Fifth Drowned. He and almost all the actors donated their fees and royalties in perpetuity to the trust set up for Caitlin and the three children.

1955
Commissioned by Tom Hopkinson, now features editor at the *News Chronicle*, Ormond's first verses were published in January, under the generic title "Saturday Picture". An image – chosen by Hopkinson, often by some of the great names of photography, among them Henri Cartier-Bresson and Bill Brandt – arrived by post every week and Ormond had to

send his words back post-haste. The by-lines of photographer and writer were given equal status: his credit was Verse by John Ormond. Clearly not considering them to be poetry in the sense to which he aspired, using the word verse was the cue for them to be virtually ignored, by him as much as anyone else. But the observations of human nature, as well as an element of gentle humour – not without its place in the tenor of a popular weekend page – flexed muscles mostly assumed to have developed unbidden in the mid-sixties. Ormond went on contributing verses whenever required, almost every week, for the next two and a half years. Decades later, when asked to name the most important influence on his life, Ormond's response was unequivocal: Tom Hopkinson. While the principles enshrined by Hopkinson at *Picture Post* were fundamental to the discipline he consciously developed at the magazine and would, in due course, apply to his film-making, the *News Chronicle* verses seem also to have played their part in his moving towards a greater simplicity and clarity of expression. In the spring, Ormond was appointed to the fledgling BBC news service in Wales, C. Day Lewis (later Poet Laureate) was one of his referees. In July, the family moved to Cardiff and the "strong, white house" in Conway Road. The fact that its high gable was decorated with a laurel wreath in bas-relief may have felt like good augury.

1956
News work proved hectic, but occasionally afforded opportunities to pursue some of Ormond's own interests, as when his concern for architecture could be reflected in a television interview with Frank Lloyd Wright on his visit to Wales in July.

1957
Ormond relinquished the *News Chronicle* commitment on being appointed as head of the newly-formed BBC Welsh Film Unit. Theirs was a small, ram-shackle building next to the river Taff, prone to flooding, now on the perimeter of the Millennium Stadium. But, already making programme on social issues, Ormond was soon looking at ideas for documentary films.

1958
Branwen was born in May, "late bud on the marriage-tree" as he wrote in an unpublished poem to her.

1960
A Sort of Welcome to Spring had earlier marked Ormond's first official venture in the film medium; the second, *Borrowed Pasture*, the portrait of two Polish farmers struggling to work derelict land in Carmarthenshire, immediately established him as a film-maker. His commentary was narrat-ed by Richard Burton and the film was shown at the Edinburgh Film Festival the following year. It would gain him the respect and friendship of John Grierson, recognised as the father of documentary film. Grierson had set up a base in Cardiff, producing and presenting his famous series for

Scottish Television, *This Wonderful World*, on which Glenys worked for him as researcher.

1961

Ormond's appointment as a senior documentary producer and director at the BBC saw the beginning of more than two decades of programme-making, recognised for its perception and sensitivity. Known, sometimes cursed, for painstakingly setting up every single shot, his experience of the *Picture Post* aesthetic came into its own. His poetic voice was most obviously channelled into writing commentaries, but his fundamental concern for structure meant that, in many respects, he approached film-making exactly as he did his poems. Significantly though, the subjects of some films would demand a more philosophical perspective that could only be realised to his satisfaction in poetry.

1962

Filming in Patagonia for his award-winning documentary *The Desert and the Dream* proved an unforgettable experience, both the landscape and its people made a deep impression. Ormond had always been proud of his Welsh identity: this trip reinforced that and, ironically, his Welsh. Before going, he had diligently bought Linguaphone's South American Spanish discs; in the event, conversations in Welsh proved more fruitful. Poems came out later; he also worked on a radio play set out on the pampas, but did not complete it.

1963

A visit to Italy filming for *A Town in Tuscany* would provide the image for his poem, 'Cathedral Builders' – written some two years later – and sowed the seeds for what – nearly two decades later – would become a profound love for the country.

1964

Return Journey was the story of Dylan Thomas's radio broadcast of the same name, the first of Ormond's three films on Thomas over the space of eighteen years. His study of the different religions of the immigrant communities in Cardiff followed very much the approach he had learned at *Picture Post*.

1965

In December, the death of Ormond's mother at home in Dunvant set in train a conscious revisiting of his home village and his early life. Though the poem dealing with his experience of the actual night of her death would not emerge for almost a decade, the process of grieving was clearly allied to Ormond's renewed sense that poetry was his real medium of expression.

1966

The publication of 'Cathedral Builders' in *Poetry Wales* marked what was seen as Ormond's return to writing and, over time, it would prove his best-loved, most anthologised, poem. Curiously, what was effectively his first film, *Borrowed Pasture*, is also seen as having been his most important and, in some ways, he regarded these successes — to which one might add the early publication of *Indications* — as burdens to be shouldered ever after. But, in the same year, his films on Vernon Watkins and Kyffin Williams established what would become a long series of portraits of creative Welshmen. They mostly happened to be friends of his; for that reason he initially resisted making them, but recognised that he was probably better placed than others to do so. For their part, his subjects found it rewarding to work with someone with whom they felt could talk on an equal artistic basis.

1967
On the recommendation of John Grierson, Ormond went to Montreal to work for the National Film Board of Canada. His film *Madawaska Valley* was concerned with issues of poverty and survival, set against the stunning beauty of the Ontario landscape in the depths of winter. His time there was not straightforward. On returning home to Cardiff, he found it difficult to settle, but threw himself into the research and filming of *Piano with Many Strings*, his portrait of the artist Ceri Richards.

1968
As a socialist and pacifist, and always politically engaged, Ormond could not be unaffected by the events of this turbulent year, yet they may have helped him gain a perspective on his own life. By the autumn, he was achieving a better balance of professional and family life and, crucially, an acceptance of his own basic identity as a poet.

1969
The filming of *The Ancient Kingdoms* had begun as professional duty – one of the BBC's programmes marking the Investiture of Prince Charles as Prince of Wales – but Ormond's immersion in the early history of Wales struck chords which over time resulted in many poems. *Requiem and Celebration*, his first collection for 26 years, was published by Christopher Davies and was well received.

1971
The Ancient Kingdoms also provided the impetus for the first of two series of films entitled *The Land Remembers*, which saw a close working partnership with the academic and poet Gwyn Williams. Meanwhile, friendship with poets Leslie Norris and Ted Walker, who lived near each other in Sussex, would prove stimulating as well as convivial. His friendships with Dannie Abse and, despite the disparity in age, with Glyn Jones, would also be significant.

1972
Ormond's portrait *R.S. Thomas: Priest and Poet* was broadcast on Easter Sunday. During the filming process, their lengthy discussions and his discovery of Thomas's slightly heretical view of Christianity may have helped

confirm Ormond in his rejection of the firm faith of his youth.

1973

Definition of a Waterfall was published by Oxford University Press and met with critical acclaim, Ormond undertaking public readings as part of the book's promotion. The birth of a grandson had also marked a milestone. His relationship with Ceri and grand-daughter Branwen would be close and the fact that they were brought up in Welsh, speaking only Welsh with Glenys, meant that he too made efforts to speak the language with them, though he saw his role as instilling perfect English.

1974

The success of the O.U.P. volume led to a Welsh Arts Council Bursary and the decision to take a year's unpaid leave from the BBC. Ormond accepted an invitation to go to the United States for the autumn's American Poetry Reading Circuit, doing sixteen readings in eleven colleges from Wesleyan, Connecticut, to Salt Lake City. Despite a slightly stuttery delivery in conversation, Ormond was a fluent and acclaimed reader of poetry, his own and that of others, his introductions illuminating and often amusing. The American visit would inspire poems, and work on an autobiographical work progressed, though ultimately not well enough, in his judgement, to pursue publication.

1975

Ormond was awarded the Cholmondley Prize for Poetry. He was invited to guest-edit a special Welsh issue of *Aquarius*, the poetry magazine founded by Eddie Linden.

1976

The filming of Ormond's portrait of the artist Graham Sutherland (1903-80) saw the beginning of an important, though all too brief, friendship.

1977

Ormond's film, *The Life and Death of Picture Post*, thirty years after its final edition, was testament to the part the magazine had played in the politics and culture of mid-20th century Britain. It was also tacit homage to the part it had played in Ormond's own career. While he and Tom Hopkinson, *Picture Post's* pioneering editor, had remained in touch through the years, the friendship was renewed after Hopkinson came to Cardiff in 1970 to set up the School of Journalism at the university.

1979

After several years' delay, Ormond's work appeared in the *Penguin Modern Poets 27* with that of Emyr Humphries and John Tripp. Ormond was one of three poets representing Britain to go to Struga in Macedonia, then still in the former Yugoslavia, to take part in the town's celebrated Poetry Evenings.

1980

Graham Sutherland died after a short illness and in April Ormond gave the address at his memorial service at Westminster Cathedral. The series *Poems in their Place* became the most specific instance of the dual career; among the contributors were John Wain on A.E. Housman and John Arlott on Edward Thomas, while Seamus Heaney's involvement in the programme on W.B. Yeats would later have an unexpected benefit.

1981

Ormond returned to Italy for the first time in 18 years. Intent on searching out a vista cherished in the memory ever since his 1963 visit, he returned to Castiglion Fiorentino, south-east of Florence. A chance recommendation sent him on to nearby Cortona: here, he found the place which, over the next few years, for just three or so weeks every summer, would become a kind of spiritual home and the source of more poetry. Towards the end of the year, he recorded a programme in BBC Radio 3 series 'The Living Poet', with the first of these Italian poems among the ones he read.

1982

On St. David's Day, Ormond read at the service of dedication at Westminster Abbey where a memorial to Dylan Thomas had been installed at Poets' Corner. U.S. president Jimmy Carter had highlighted the absence of one and, around the same time, Ormond had lobbied and set up a subscription fund collecting from friends, colleagues and fellow-poets; the fund went towards commissioning sculptor Jonah Jones to carve in green Welsh slate the words from Thomas's poem 'Fern Hill': *Time held me green and dying/ Though I sang in my chains like the sea.* Ormond's final film on Dylan Thomas, *I Sing to you Strangers*, broadcast later that year, sought to look at the real Dylan through the eyes of friends and contemporaries. Through his long association with Michael Collins of Washington's Georgetown University, a loyal champion of his work, Ormond had again been invited to read at Georgetown's summer programme in Fiesole. It was this connection, together with the generosity of writer Robert Williams who had a home in Cortona, that made the visits viable. While going there was in some ways an almost romantic conceit, the small medieval city seemed to unlock something in his psyche. He felt welcome, a feeling helped in no small way by the general euphoria of Italy's progress towards winning the 1982 World Cup, and the particular camaraderie at the Bar Sport, later named Caffè Vittoria. It all proved conducive to writing, and as well as poems, he tackled again the story of the re-burial of Yeats's body which he'd first done at *Picture Post*. In December, Ormond delivered the W.D. Thomas Memorial Lecture at Swansea University on the subject of Wallace Stevens, the invitation in itself a turn of events he could hardly have envisaged when himself the object of Professor Thomas's displeasure 40 years before.

1983

Retirement from the BBC at 60 was intended to allow Ormond to focus on poetry and writing. In the event, he also contributed regularly to radio programmes, produced columns for the *Western Mail* and also lectured at Cardiff University's School of Journalism. Once again, his weeks in Italy in the summer were both pleasure and self-imposed exile: the sense of community he enjoyed there was countered by his missing home, both factors implicit in the writing process. By the end of the year, Ormond and his wife went back to Italy to house-sit high in the hills outside Florence, this time a four-month stay which further deepened his affinity with the place.

1984

Bitten by a tick during that Italian winter, Ormond developed Lyme Disease, hitherto not identified as such in Britain, so that a long succession of medical tests on his return to Cardiff would only prove negative. The manner of its eventual diagnosis came about by chance the following year: the Irish-American specialist in tropical medicine, Dr. Kevin Cahill, had been recommended by Seamus Heaney to contact Ormond about Dylan Thomas. This may have added a suitably poetic final flourish to the story, but suffering the characteristic symptoms of malaria-like, cyclic fevers and debilitating rheumatic pains made it a rough time. During all this, Ormond nevertheless succeeded in writing and speaking the commentaries for a series of seven 50-minute documentaries about the earth's ecology from the earliest times, directed by his friend and BBC colleague Brian Turvey. The themes of *Far From Paradise* resonated with Ormond's own perceptions of land and landscape, inspiring a script that was both poetic and philosophical. The work also triggered ideas for poems, only some of which would be pursued.

1986

Almost two years after the tick-bite, treatment with millions of units of intravenous antibiotics finally killed the Lyme Disease. Hooked up at Cardiff Royal Infirmary's William Diamond ward, nicknamed 'Willie Die', Ormond was relieved to joke that now he wouldn't, but, compounded by the onset of diabetes, the illness had taken its toll. Italy provided the tonic he needed during the summer. He wrote 'Tuscan Cypresses' and began assembling the poems for his next collection.

1987

In May, *Selected Poems* appeared under the Poetry Wales Press imprint to further acclaim. Two months later, Ormond was made an Honorary Fellow of the University of Swansea. The Gregynog Press, known for the quality of its printing, also proposed a volume of his poetry. Ormond, always fastidious about the planning and design of every detail of his own books, was thrilled to work on the Gregynog book, not least since it was envisaged that he would do his own illustrations. Delays at the press meant it was only after his death that the volume was published.

1988

The Italian summer sojourn was cut short when Ormond suffered what was probably a slight stroke, though he tried to make light of it. He was fortunate to overcome the episode without too many problems but, psychologically, it was another setback.

1989

Seren published the *Selected Poems* of John Tripp, which Ormond had edited. Tripp's death in 1986 robbed Ormond of a friend whose sharp wit he had enjoyed sharing, as well as his acerbic view of the literary scene occasionally expressed in the skittish, unpublished and doubtless unpublishable, leaves of a magazine they called "Poetry Whitchurch" (the city suburb where Tripp and Glyn Jones lived). Marking Georgetown University's Bicentennial, Ormond was honoured to be one of four recipients of the commemorative Bicentennial Medal. For the first time, he was not able to make the pilgrimage to Italy and, instead, Michael Collins came to Cardiff to make the presentation. But Ormond continued to work on poems and to make plans for a new collection.

1990

In late April, Ormond suffered a stroke. At his bedside in hospital, Glenys was astonished at the reams of poetry – Shakespeare, Yeats, Thomas and countless others – that he recited in a sort of fevered incantation, as though aware that he should keep his brain functioning. Initially such signs suggested a recovery but, over twelve days, his condition gradually deteriorated and he died on 4 May. At his memorial service in Llandaff Cathedral on 25 May, Dai Smith and Alun Richards spoke the eulogies, with Ted Walker and Dannie Abse among those who read poems in tribute.

1991

The Gregynog Press published *Cathedral Builders and Other Poems*, almost exactly as Ormond had originally intended, but using drawings done for Glenys in a copy of his *Selected Poems*, emulating Ceri Richards's illustrations of pages of Dylan Thomas's *Collected Poems*, a gift for his wife Frances.

1992

On May 18, a commemorative plaque, inscribed with the last two lines of his poem 'The Gift', was dedicated to Ormond at Georgetown's Villa le Balze in Fiesole.

1997

A plaque, carved by the artist/craftsman Ieuan Rees – one of a series of slate plaques commemorating Welsh writers erected under the auspices of the Welsh Academy and the Rhys Davies Society – was unveiled on the house in Conway Road by Ormond's friend, the artist Kyffin Williams. The plaque's simple design was chosen to complement the poet's laurels at the top of the house, its inscription reading: John Ormond Poet 1923-1990.

I

Poem in February

Walking beside the lank sea-shore in February
with the faint birdmarks, triangular,
and the grave curl and cry of the whirlpool bay,
I set a line the wave cannot destroy,
wave turning upon the dunes, beyond the rock
first searched and sought out by the renewing tide
that leaves no hidden sanctuary.

The line is valid as a winter dream; upon no rack of logic
under the print of nails, proving some non-existence
of a spirit by a manrib cracking before pain;
it is no wreck of a ghostship on the shore,
gone in the daylight, only there in moon;

so when the reedwinds come to seek me out
my hair is seagrass, fingers sand,
and over all the watermarks they pass;
there is no enemy; here is friend.

The slender sun combing the gray hair's cloud
drops the insistent shadow on the distant castle;
broken like bone. Yet on the beach the skull's no alien,
and the black woods around above witness no burial
of the dead seas. They are not alone

for under them all and the leaf-moulds, and the waters
through the late winter boughs, and under the stones,
the skull and I are handlocked like a flood,
a flood in February when first the primrose breaks.

Three Sonnets from a Cycle

I

Sentinel to the soul, the unthrenodic finger
directs the candlelight to the green centre
from whence grows up the patterned frequency
of my sun-coloured doing; falling upon
the silent extending root and primrose
the fears are bared and known, the red-throated leaf
– the frames of faith have knowledge as they fall
in a decaying dance to the music-barren grave.
Across the mind's mountains you struggle on
with the reports and paper eyes, neglecting
your own hands' magnet, the clear direction
given you in your hair, the leaves that never fall.
Sitting in shadow at the receipt of custom, the gold
shining upon the tables as you perish.

II

Give me no insecure, heraldic flower
to kill my hand, to wound the hour I live
fatally within my core, letting me walk on
alone, waiting for the crumbling of the shell;
for I must bury my face within the folded blossoms
growing in disarrangements from the eye's tree.
the leaves having no identity, essence
of the beggar liberty, the poet tongue.
Here is the common light and I the prism
twist at the white and give to it its lustre.
You are the midwives at the birth of love
that is the river's wind and citadel.
You are the children of the tattered rent-book
who have been left upon some winter steps.

III

My love grow pregnant, wane and rise again
to mark the graph upon the memory
that holds as long as the mapped hand remains
the line that's useless to the loveless dead;
that pulls at will of the sufficient fruit
out of the granite, ever-foetal branch,
that closes stiff as soon as needing's done,
locks itself up, will not receive again.
I know our difference woman in my side,
but the white-turreted bridge that holds us
is not the only spirit at our bodies' table;
not the vague turret and the sky within the mind
within the symbol and the marginned note
but the hard tower and the actual cloud.

Direction

I set out past all heads
to a place where hands are rulers,
where actions are understood
through the medium of unseen gropings;

to a city of seconds, not
of charted eras and maps,
only to the pattern of an island
marked by the contours of a body.

All time is the present
and the past is but the growth
to the eternal peak moment
upon which I can now place my finger.

No future is there to be
but the next movement that grows
like light from the dying present.
No death is there but the changing minute.

Only my heart is the clock;
only my blood grinds the shores
of trouble; only my breathing
is the wind that blows death into leaves in autumn.

Procession

Vespers of widows, breathing knived,
echo with water in its clutch of fame
under departing branches where the rain
dissolves the flesh of little ones away.
There with their graves of eyes
the young men bend and fancy
their faces with the eyes of youths.
O, they are old. For each blue mark
upon their gray-veined bodies
there is a lash across their heart.

Fastened together by red rusting whips
and mandril's sound upon the rock,
they tie their common ribbon
to the rough-cut granite cross.

Gentle the ring of light within the stall
a soft gleam in the shroud of his father
where the coal-face glowers.

They move in the procession of leaves
across the hill's shoulder,
down the arm of the coarse road
and weep their hymns above the hand
of the grave
found in the straying sinew of the earth.

And the corners of their mouths struggle
when as white weeds in the dark
they slip with their thin breathing, quick
to the absent end.

I, at the Channel

I, at the channel of my windowsill
flow down the circles of the coloured pool
and cut strange steps into the will of hope
that rises in the huge misshapen wave.

Out of the weakness of my regular arms
the stringent tides stretch out the body, tie
the moving of the sea at my finger-tips
to the student trees at the breast of the earth I sucked.

The rains of sufferance and the knives' return
come to my head and pin the hair
flat to the sea and to the waters' edge:
and wicks of time soak slowly to their grave.

And at my feet my coffin weight of love
rots in the canvas shroud, where starfish move
vague in the light, between the native boats,
that plumbs the greenness of my tropic sea.

And through the rotting of my seaweed side
I feel the stitching up my quiet limb
ease with the thought of slipping now away
to peace. A great beginning.

Bright Candle, my Soul

Bright candle, my soul of steel,
break through the edges of the failures past;
reflect, now the loud wind and rain
have blown so far into the receptive land
all light in the dark direction
we have come, conquered,
yet somehow failed.

Break love, as credit slowly;
wither the will of the doomed;
love, break in a straighter forward wheel.
Come, patient as the sower
on the stone ground, dream not.
Whiten you knuckles if your new will
turn face in any weird light, but walk
walk steadily and do not wane.

In your deep bones you feel it; the pen
wriggles a song in any hand, but
feel the diamond in the earth's dull centre
and light will break through any rock of paper.

You feel its blood, for it is forever there.
It is the tooth's nerve, the lover's clean eye,
the fingernail's growing and the fingers
lifting bread to a mouth. It is the green river.

Bright candle, my soul of steel
break through the edges of the failures past;
reflect on the strings of winter lace;
river-reeds' hair, my snow, delicate
fair shoulder towards the firm cold,
foot in the white, lined furrow,
ear to the field's side's song.

Take the skull's sky and weave
black branches winter lace;
that gray veins' labyrinth
sharpening the ancient mountain,
pointing the myth.

Burn clear, send on
all glances through a purer prism.

The Symbols

for Eileen

Now these twin candles with circled rings of light
fortify each other and uphold the darkness:
powerful as guns, meek as the altar tapers
they guard the living at the sepulchre.

Coming into my room from the irksome hill
my spirit is adjusted to the marriage
and the strong centres of their unity
draw in my shoulders to the core

of their vitality and all their being.
I can never detach myself for a second, only
half-hide myself for a short while, on the edges
of the outer darkness, to know their inward power.

Poem at the Beginning of Winter, 1942

for Alex Comfort

I

One are the root and the sun that hold
the erect tower and the living tree;
a season's gold is measured by the self-same foot
as the sea and the flowering hillock.

From under the gray street and wall
probes down out of the day's eye
the unmarried blossom of the warmest bosom
and the tall globe and the uncharted thunder
grow from the heart of the single earth-shawl.

One is the piteous autumn leaf and the gold
of the dark earth and the night's yellow stars;
where life stirs, like a needle, haggard, stark
as the broken mirror in the bombed house
with naked, piercing light, is the same
fact as the singing richness of the unknown peace.

The indifferent stone and the one-sided feud
have no knowledge of their virgin bride
but sleep, they feel, alone. Grief has become
afferent only, does not return to the fringe
of this unbrooding oblivion where lie the lately dead.

My blood is the same warm river as the tide
that surges across the balance of the mountain;
the storm and flood of all relief and credence
open as wide as ever upon both songs and dirges
of the world that holds their life and death.

I cannot measure the quantity of each
and set the forces in stones against each other;
they work in every mind and jet of water,
and the leaves turn their faces in summer

along the same line, towards the only east,
although the guns facing the uglier others
fire across another treacherous channel.

II

Upon the black wild wave
the dead falter to-night's losses
and the notes of grief string inward
towards the gray-wooded silent shore.

Patience at broken, gutted windows
is ousted by pain, and the mind
is drilled hollow and the filling
remains in the sea's black cowardice.

Weeping is useless, the dry burning
of eyes waits and is disappointed,
for the gray sand's clutch is heavy
and the decaying water
too deep for the brittle bone to return
with a message of recoverance.

Pain, constant at the window is not killed
by a patriot's silencer
and a tin mould's reward
fails to put up a solid front of bravery.

And the fear remains
behind the futile shell of hope, where
the sea has entered the fixed mouth
and salt cakes in the throat.

★ ★ ★

Against the tide, pain travels
inwards towards the land
and sucks at the living hearts
that are dead out in the Atlantic.

III

Therefore it is not easy, friend,
it is not easy to say:
There must be an end,
There comes a day
When the wind shall cease
To blow us malice.
For new corn can grow
only if soil and seed are willing
and it is no use filling
a broken chalice.

I have seen the shadow
of this young, gray ship of new winter
flow into the sea of the fourth year.
Off autumn's chaotic stocks
I saw it go; they are bereft
of everything save what we made.
Dark stains are left
on the throat of another decade.
I have nothing but fear.

No, not even a dog licks
the same old sores for ever.
They are too sour for even his tongue,
And sometimes the body lives too long.

The flowers placed within the room of faith
smell sweet in youth;
now they have grown, they have sharp stalks. The devil
for whom we are not responsible
makes them smell bitter, evil.

The flowers, I admit are paler
by the red sky of war.
Let us keep them alive
for they will be needed.
I fear, if you have a loaf
over, it will be required.

Yes, sometimes the body lives too long.
Flowers are no use to the dead.
It is for us to wed faith to the living.

Let our compass be beneath us, the coal,
stone of time's experience.
We must not allow the toll of indefinite grief
to be paid for a few years' sluggishness.

Let us take hope, friend, such nightingale
as sings for us cannot always fail.
But remember, we have in front a task
uncertain, weird as any bergamask,
and sores grow bitter for a single tongue.

Sometimes the body lives too long,
Sometimes the body dies too young.

Towards the End of a Winter

The water passes through me
rotting my tongue,
from the clouds of my soul
they have wrung
the rains of repentance.

With beauty past and dead
around the forest's face
and in the aching hill
and lines of age...

This is my face
and the water falling.
Alas for the age in my hair
and the trees in winter.

And the rain withering through me
taking me away,
taking me away
to the ground
in the cassock of water.

We Have no Name

We have no name, there is no iron wall
between us and the sky and our crushed forests;
and we are found the keeper and the riders
essential to any roundabout of worlds.

The evening star rises and falls about us
the constant North, and the arms of spring
fold in around us and grow yellow with unborn
seasons that overtake from under the horizon
gently with the twilight, earlier in the autumn.

Mother of the phoenix ashes wet with tears of Wales
we are, and after the said rains
when the last sacrament between our hairs and hearts
lies self-adjusted, to the mountains, to the fingers
we return, in the quick balancing we go
when the torrent has abated.

After the old men have told, preconceived
the treaties are written out full on our foreheads,
we go to their age, to the November skies
not to their words but to their saffroned faces.
After the sages have measured the distances
the old truth remains and the breast is as rounded,
the traffic of death goes past our high windows
and the hands of the poor still knock at our doors,

telling that theirs is the house and we are the beggars
that after the gospels the meal is our business
laid on the clean table for anyman's bastard,
the sacrament formed by the eye is the compass
the hand is the mind that grafts the two branches.

Before the Peace to Be

Though under a strange new paper the bough
straight as a spire, makes no spear, only
that the blood throws it up to the sky,
but it does not fall in our time only by the knife
and so the springtime is not mercenary,

and even though the bud appear arrow, and the sun
at evening lend a red poison to the tip of cancerous green,
flow the peaceful stars through the quiet water's heaven,
the same soil and soul run under Europe.

Wait for the first nominal peace of autumn, and
the same skirl of leaves, driven by the same foot
shatters the hillside like a globe on a tree at Christmas,
and the same winter creeps up along November
white in the gentle frost given by shortening days.

Second Epithalamion: Madonna and Child

I

How can I help but create
a beautiful boy-image of our first son
when the ideal is fashioned in our brain
and you my clay model perfection?

He shall have eyes as dark as yours
whose depths are agents of my vision
to give me words, as to the climbing hawk
the unvoiced heights give insight to the talon.

He shall have hands of poetry, and
all the roots of earth shall forfeit to his mind
the mounting scents' and saps' maturity,

for you whose fragrance is the lilac's
in the white praying of the first April day
hold in your veins the blood of our first son
as beautifully as the ebbing of a sea.

II

In coalescence, seed through seed,
veins separately through a single blood
dictate a harvest. Sense
and its graph locked in the twisting rain
and furrowed sunshine underneath a stream
where mood flows into word.

Better is waiting; fragile handling
of the bud holds the firm flower and granary;
future to tap the pane where glass holds out
the touching of a room that's understood.

Those winds are best, my little one, to scatter
the smashing petal-grains across the frame
where wheat is growing on the inner sill
and the first stalk kisses the stretching fingers.

III

From this, our embryonic flame,
admitting not even star-felt threnody,
light grows illuminating the heart's dome
with plumes out of an empyreal day.

Here is the only vast cathedral
lit by a single sacrifice
of self to self, when, in a moment, all
worlds are in a lover's face;

when, by a taper of identity,
outside the wick that holds our past,
the fats are merged in chastity of intercourse;
and self is lost,

till all the windows in the farthest wall
live and project their figures in the sun
by the single flame, and the tall
saints quit the glass to walk the world:
      thus He is risen.

Before the Saps Descended

Before the saps descended into fern and fossil,
long first my fathers, my tubed brain
was fashioned like an undivided bird's,
building then knowing beak.

Once long the forests pushed the coal
(a tree is and the bright sky's blue)
into our lands and through our married eyes;
we had our children, then we knew their heads.

I knew I did. The road upon my temple
made me see lines, and knives made blood;
the beard-grass made bread, occasional black stones
made fire that warmed; roasted; frightened wolves.

Elegaic Nocturne

Not quiet lying and lulled by the falling season
grows to the candle, the green bough turning
into the four-walled courtyard below the empty window.

Nor the wind's dim drum, nor the unseen tapping
tapping on the wall in the long ivy's hand nor
the star's faith nor the night taper below mourning
below, far below mourning and the eyes burning away.

Death is as cold in June; north is as sure
under cap and cloud, October and bean-flower
blossoming at night, falling in certainty of
a fallow month. Sleep as wasteful for the diseased,

Upon the taut flagstone the draught wears thin
the plate of funeral tears, fallen a month,
scoured every day and remaining flood upon flood,
word upon word, faith upon faith, tree upon tree.

I breathe now, or do I sleep and it is she
in the night encompassing the dark? I
am the centre and circumference, and the
vast and unique sea and grain of sand
is in my blood and bone, the always price of corn.

Strange Within the Dividing...

Strange within the dividing of blood-lines
   the doubt of a relegation of spirit is born,
The wet moonlit grasses with their tasteless wines
   wait for to-morrow and the dawn,
While the hollow questions have echoed through sleep,
   On, plunging down past colourless green,
   Towards the raining morning,
     in which with its grey half-mourning
Now as always they will keep
   asking the clutching, Where have we been?
   Where have we been?

Always the night has covered the track,
   tossing the traces with the blue cloud sand
Taking love's twigs and heather in her dark hand
and making a new bed in the low rock,
   Under whose shadow with their cold walk
   they may hide the straw enclosed leaf,
Red with the blood of unfathomable grief
   Holding up towards the hanging branch a brow
   wet with the eagerness of the creation
     and again cooling with the vow
   pledging the war of condemnation.
Never to be forgotten, only to break
   with the ultimate gain of freedom's sake.

Funeral of a German Airman

(whose body was washed up on the South Wales coast 1943)

Though smothered under your flag, as all soldiers
        are smothered, limbs irresistibly tied
by the knots of no-cause and all-too-certain death,
I say your heart is still in flower
shedding this futile badge, as futile as our crosses.

Before the fishes came the kind waves –
the day before your death as alien as England
– bore you onto an enemy but a friendly shore
for a quiet place in solid soil, instead of
your body searching the seas blindly for a grave.

British bullets fire over now, not into your body
as you lie in a strange but as scented a bed
as any man has a right to expect, as undisturbed
as any man who perhaps at the point of a gun
had a gun placed in his hand.

Birthday Poem

I give you for your birthday night
a poem to lay your head upon.

Dream softly, as the waterfall
darkly descends, of the remotest
moments, dim in their beginnings, lit
by the nearest sunlight in the green
rocks of water, purple weeds
under the cave and hill
of happiness. In the last haven,
an ultimate image, see the past
moving. Watch with me,
regard the separate figures, that, brought
in separate drops, stalactites compose
under the flood and undistinguishable
stamens of hanging time, the single
yellow flower, joined in the latticed pool
you sleep in. Beneath the surface
nothing seems but sands and grasses,
dead chrome and greens; and when
first I watched I did not understand.
Yet as light fails, and the heat-haze
is stilled, the confusing colours
of sun dwindle and their meaning
is projected, predominating blue
of penetration, the mind (holding
the memory's colour) distinguishes
all that remains from all that passes on.
So in late evening, the elegy
of day asserts itself; and knowing
we are breathing we make the most of breath.
At last, at night-time, when falls
the perfect rain upon her waters
the flame upon her grave diminishes;
the fevered leaf, the quiver
of satiated summer, is calmed,

and the trembling ceases. Then
I move under the boughs (still
this beneath her voice), darkened
with certain evening, not with sorrow,
following a strange dancer, who
only half known, is loved for separate
movements that her dance discloses.
Her hair is dark as hers, but
her eyes avoid me, as eyes of a madonna
in alabaster, ever cast down.
Her dancing can be mistaken
for the gentle rain. The whisper
of my eyes upon her
gives out my argument.
> *Renewing palimpsest*
> *of rose on rose; the petals*
> *grow more of night.*
The dancers (sometimes the one
and then, as from two flames,
another, but always
the single loved one) more beautiful
in consciousness of beauty's
seeming to pass. And as the rose in water
(the weeds have faded first,
then taken on their mineral) more
beautiful imprisoned in a glass
causing reflection, the many
dancers to one bud and revealing,
that broken do not crumble
but remain in the same sweet dust
and in the ancient kiss.
And Juliet is refuted: the single budding
birthday, and the nothing after;
the one, and only
one turning of the leaf.

The tale goes on, the dancer, the
inevitable seed in the illumination
of body's parchment bursts forth,

the letters sprout, the word,
the language of the dance begins
and the night ends in the expected dream.
Risen an hour the young moon
sinks; day's recompense begins;
but before daylight, and ultimately
noon, we watch the flame burn
through the floral moment,
the moving monument that stands
naked in the land
of the living; and the root
wreathed round the realising heart
moves silently as in the deepest soil.
Only the flame, the flower
unashamed, burning perpetually
for use who watch beneath the pool
of the occasional glance and word,
reveals the first smile after
a terrible sorrow is upon youthful lips
as the yellow sun upon features faded
of invalids and aged. The flame
burns on: sleep, sleep in the quiet
light of it. The new flower
grows. Lay down your head and sleep.
And the cataract break
through the rock and hillside's colour:
a star has fallen, an immeasurable,
deeply into the pool. The tides,
the long tides probe the equinox.
As one strand of fallen necklace
of summer's stream, this star has fallen,
has left its pearl, as dew, at the heart
of the night's dark and all-enclosing flower.
We are without hope to stay
a single season; yet the shades
of fern and forest last.
Outside the hill-horizon withers.
The birds are silent as a younger sleep
than yours. The pool has disappeared.
The rivers of our world

are more profound. The rock drifts
her turret in the cloud: her statues
lean farther forward in their pose.
The silver rose contracts.
The tree's dumb rhetoric
invades the skull. Darkness
distils the last thought.
Is it the final whisper of the pool
in the recipient shell?
Is it the dancer speaks?
Once more
the rain begins to fall.

Now sleep, the cataract, fall softly
upon your dreams of the first birth
and of the most recent day: over
the pine-wooded hills of the night
may you wander, and see
the inland pools of yesterday and to-day.
May the perceptive star unravel
the intricate, coloured weeks
(in water that will travel
away tom-morrow) and your dreads
of the hidden stone, and the tall
green twisted shadow under the waterfall.
Before you wake, may you enter
the cave I sleep in, in all
months, even when snow in winter
annihilates the colours of the fall,
and in silence realise the peace
I seek, I find within your face.
May you in dreaming recognise
the dream I have of after sunset,
when he who listens knows
the water speaks, and says the sight
is never dimmed, that the silver rose
only contracts until the sun arise.
Each dropping moment, carrying the seed
of perfect happiness, assembles

into love's stalactite; the sad
death that others see does not affect, it trembles
and dies itself. Time is withheld,
its jewels hand in stone, fold upon fold.
As the cut flower in water is
lovelier since it blooms but once,
though each day that passes loses
its first petals, the concentrated glance,
the object and reflection of its beauty
gives second sight supreme reality.
In the dancer that I always see
dance on the stage of the sleeping wind
may you behold that immortality,
transcendent figure, flame, perpetual in the mind,
and realise the dancer is your image
reflected in poem's crystal hermitage.

Selections from An Elegy for Alun Lewis

I

Who sees the white saps rise
     in the ash-tree's thigh
has breathed earth's day
and in his vision has created:

Who holds in mind, perpetually,
the struggle between thorn and flower
has seen the living enmity
Within the stone; and truce

can never be: who sees, in men
on coaltips, and in dancing rivers
the feud of time, and for the dead
of this unending duel, the dirge
of the yellow stars, fertile,
evanescent, that flare in contradiction
as crocus buds in February.
Now, untouchable, remote
as their embroidery on blue
he lies, surpassing truth
that he created. *But we
will fail to touch validity.*

II

Poets are few, and those who fall
into the unmeasured, almost
unpremeditated darkness
forestall their vision, as fliers
at night seeking the unblemished north
with instruments not perfectly adjusted.

They fall too soon to identify
the code, as we, who remain,
do not possess their log, who saw
the secret for so short an instant
to tell the path – the shadow
would not wait upon their eyes.

We can but move towards the unaltering light
by implications from their discarded premises.
We shall not know if any logic holds.

III

Through many requiems, and gentle summers
and autumns, when the seeds
of secret love burn and are lost in Wales,
his grave will wait for snow
that in our winter valleys covers the tilted fields
where as a boy he learned to be a poet.
Through the ecstatic moments, movements
of futurity, cleanly without pretension
he trod, and then looked back, and worded
his path with certainty, deliberation,

But death, the antithesis
of snowdrift (except that both
have varying depths) has not allowed
the last account of travel...

☀ ☀ ☀ Let Us Break Down the Barriers...

Let us break down the barriers of crying.
Tears cannot stretch forth their fingers
Far enough down from the shadow
Into the sunlight to grasp the trouble.
They are blistered and evaporated
Leaving no mark, and not touching
The ache that made us weep.

It is but in the crucible of meeting
In which compounded are the salts:
And happens the crystallisation of issues:
That longing is caught in the prism of the eye,
Is split up for us to see,
Is refracted out, and continues.
We are as before, except
That we have seen carved in light
For a sharp-edged moment in the sun
The nucleus of our existence, of our purpose.

If for a moment the emotion of the whole
Of all quick-thinking elements of time
Is caught within the starlit instant's glance,
Your tears are futile
As the apple-blossom in the wind,
And as insecure as the ripples
Left on the shore by the tide.

Yet I understand the mysteries of ages
Through the circle of a young child's pity.

Feed them the moment, and your unborn child
And clean the corroding water.
Strengthen the chain's link
And weld the whole around the earth...

You will not break for there runs
Throughout the flowers
A wire unbreakable in all eras of space.

First Sleep

Until the threat of April in the seed
drew me from dreaming on a singing string,
deep in the shafts of my childhood's history
a river remembered light through ferns and leaves
set in the stones by the weights of ancient summers.

When my first origin knew darkness like a star
my eyes were kissed to lust in secrecy.
Before the first I slept in the intimate waters
soothed by the tales and voices of the sea.
My ageless heart was a husk in a harvest's cage.

Last autumn's stalks and roots explored my limbs
until their picks came nearer to my tomb,
breaking my sleep, tapping upon my skull
gently, and gently leading me through stalls
where darknesses ran to gold in the living hills.

Daybreak and daydream met on the moon's bright wires
drawing the slanting heads of the daffodils.
Dusk and eventless sleep withdrew their hands
into the earth. Shaping the changeless clay
their fingers feared the flower-withering day.

From the white arms of the mountain's ancestry
I moved in love to the men with the ancient eyes,
whose bones were crossed with the bones of tragedy,
whose lips were wild with the songs of the singing flood.
And the river slept at my waking to the world.

Portrait of his Grandfather

He spoke with the prayers of widows, his breath
Pinned on the water by his boyhood's arm.
His words were psalms. In his chaptered hand
A seed of a century broke to a branch of death,
Each leaf a cross to loss in a candled dark.

Pools beyond speech mirrored his fallacy. Bending
With blue-marked face where stones in mistake
Slipped truth, the old lie trembling, he saw
Nothing but country, only the earth's firm fruit.

The coal-face glowered. Rusted wire whips,
Red with their passive anger, lashed his black hair
To white. Slowly the settled dust increased
Its sound, clinked with the mandrelled rock,
Each grain a grave for the sun when its light was locked.
The whips and wires wound him to charity.

His miracle was faith, his gospel love. Peace
Was a thing he lost. He found an utter calm
In the long fingered trees when the sap was high.
Only his heart and his father knew his ghost.

Portrait of his Mother

A collier's lamp lit the room she lived in.
The autumn leaves hung copper on the wall.
As lanterns show my craft in the muttering vein
Her craft was waiting when the night was tall.

Starlight said nothing locked in listening.
The village was still as I lay in her quiet womb.
Waiting she whispered, afraid of the quivering
Floor, shaping my name in his doom.

The darkness demanded a faith which her years denied.
Her words were of water drained from a barren well.
Only accepting the growing weight in her side
Her words were of water. Then the image fell.

By light and logic her words were afraid of birth.
By dreams they mentioned water's history.
By morning faith rose up again from earth.
The autumn leaves hung copper on a tree.

Portrait of his Father

From his gentle craft and his loins I woke
Hammered to words in the active midnight:
With care and calling in the quiet walls
The house prepared its face for my creation.

His hands made my silver bed, a boat
To sail through the falling stones, through
The dark of the visioned lands where I made
No mark, where the feet of the dying left no sounds.

The leaves grew through his hands to light
Shading the countries where my lids were closed
In the fields where summer lies; his hands were made
To break the rainbow for my waking eyes.

Where the water of April sprang in the hill
He taught me to drink the holy air;
When the fires of summer burnt the grain
He taught me to catch the breathing rain.

For the seasons of skill are older than grief
And the balancing flames in the autumn leaves;
Death has no colder words than those
Which defy the epitaphed common man.

The Unseen Blind

Under the hanging bell a secret music
rests with its head upon the iron tongue;
under the ropes of the dead, invisible ringers,
dressed in a naked image, touch the skull.
There where the living wires net the roses
they stand ensnaring sunlight in their hair;
grown old with tying summer to the branches
they speak at last outside the laughing wars.
Their voices cut no scar on peace or power,
their scarce and sacred homage makes regret
a casual gesture on rhetoric waters.
Even their certainty cannot recover
the birth love made too intricate for death.

Bright love was buried by their climbing heels
as through slow tunnels of desire they came,
Thrushes drove out their wings through the dark walls.
After they came the lilac moulded snow.
And unidentified in bitter light
that burned their cheeks with rivers of its gain
they mastered tragic theorems of decay
until their marrow knew the stars by name.
Then the bell moved with breathing in the stone.
Then the long-muttering winds hewed them a place,
out of the quarried journey of their eyes
raced up the staircases towards their home.

The bell was still. Taken, they ripped their masks
showing where day had weighed their fallen lids.
Dawn came, with it a single wren
dropped on their wrists to show them a slight dream.
They sang, and knew the last word was their last.
The least among them tore the unyielding floor.

Only the wind remembered how they came.
The light was conscious of their shape no more.
Moving their lips they found no words among them.
On the grey stone their terror whitened hair
grew green with leaves, pointing the unseen sun.
The bird flew off, which way no one could tell.
A rose struck single utterance from the bell.

For the Children, Bronwen and Neil

Blessing the innocence of your sleep I blow
the flowers back to birth, for while they grew
slow as your hooded eyes before the light
knew of its luck, before the morning came
keeping its heraldry from off your name,
your birth was known before your limbs were white.

Before the angel entrance of your head
spoke suddenly in crying the long dead
knew of your welcomed coming, the old sun,
holding the summer in a folded seed
imagining December garlanded,
counted your days of waiting one by one.

Where the stored blood saved up your infant heart
your tongue made previous utterance of the great
assembled armies of triumphal birds,
the buildings winged to kingdoms over water,
and broken into men in son and daughter,
using an eloquence impossible in words.

Blessing the innocence of your sleep I hear
your breath mark out the profile of a year,
shaping the tottering ages in a night.
Measure the future for me. May your eyes
cut with a glance the dangling rope's surmise.
Before your birth was known your limbs were white.

The Angels in the Air

I come with my homaging heart bared wide as pupil
For my listening blood to hear
The leaf or stone speak in a pulse or word
Shaped by the one still season
At the pin of the turning globe.
But I find their voices voiceless
And in their faces
See death's ill-hidden line spin out its web,
See that their veins of life or age,
Filled by the wrinkling, law-revoking weather,
Confide me nothing, nothing I did not know
Before the world, remade in dew's bright wonder,
Bore the return of innocence and light,
Met with the schools and pardons of the eyes
Bringing beatitudes to light much older,
Coursing from fountainheads no sun denies.

They in their calm send my glances flowering
Along the travelled light of the outer stars
First made as markers for the cries
Of Adam and the angels. Now I know no Adam
Only that I am here
By leaf and stone which show me silent death.
And still the eyes which look across my shoulder
Teach me invisible distances
Inched by a sand of stars.
Returning figures walk down my waiting gaze.
And men crowd in. Knowing no one of them
I see them stand, untouched by wind or sleet,
Moon or the sourcing sun,
Men out of miracles,
Meeting race-burning bursts of the blinding skies
Still and serene as dew, for swords lie at their feet.

Expectation

Waiting that naked figure winged with fire
I know that she will come,
For I have seen her walk from tortuous dream,
Enter the maze and harm of winter,
Each feather flying back
With sulphurous wing-tips spectral flame.

I followed her but lost my way
In the wound woods and suddenly alone,
Dressed in the roping snow,
Tied hard by icy down,
I could not turn to follow or cry
After her, or had I cried
My words would have all been lost
In the curls of the tumbled sky.

Yet where she disappeared
The snowskirl faltered, the ravelling
White waste of the air warmed at her wing
And at her touch a bough
Of a tree burst into green spray,
The incalculable bird began to sing.

I could believe her shape were now
Half dream, half apparition;
For now it is cold, the skies array
Smothering swarms of the snow ready for flight
To silence the world with white.

Birdsong is all a ghost; the thrush
Is silent, unable to relate
How frost falls in her flesh,
Marks her articulate note
With the syllables of cold.
But I await that ghost
Winged with a golden flame;

For at her hands
The wood waves out in wands,
The world finds a new tongue,
Nothing is dumb.
Wind wears the winter's name.
The snow begins to fall. Still she will come.

So sleep, incalculable bird,
No need for flight
Beyond this word
To tell how the world turns.
Whiteness of snow, false morning, though it come,
Though your notes may not touch the sun
They may tell how the sun burns.
Fly towards spring and spring is gone;
Light is elusive as green's secret;
So wait, and sleep; withhold your song
For that moment of the heart's heat
When words break from defeat
And dark and the snow are gone;

When autumn's forced charity,
The brass inevitable coins
That fall from grudging skies
Buy new reasons for the old tunes
That oust the work of snow
And fire the stones to speech,
And the sun's strange eyes
Watch his green aviaries
Shake and bewilder dark
And all light's enemies,
The naked figure loiter through the trees.

Ikon

Mary Madonna: see, they are not his eyes,
Nor are they yours.
                    Out of the world's hurt,
This time, the hollow of your heart,
From a miraculous tree this winter rose
Is born.
            His eyelids close. Serenely
Gaze upon his face. Again he is far
In a country you have never seen.
Nor will you see it, Mary Madonna.

He is the casual inheritor of your blood
But keep him warm from the elaborate and
Contriving cold.
                Look how he moves his hand,
Would touch you. Turn him towards your breast,

Suckle his strange ghost. Then rest,

Prepare for a journey. Make ready the child
Under your stars for the night ride.

Windsor Forest Fall

In such a place as this the world is altered,
Where two ways intermix and the wild leaves drive apart.
It changes as it falters on a sound
Framing the season's litter as the one wind
Heaps it around the stones and frosted trees,
As it searches those images time has left haltered
In the winterbarred and prisoning ground
To hold blood's secrets, earth's realities,
When the rising, falling stream threads the reflecting heart.

Here between pulse and pulse the new spring enters
Her constant channels, waiting new flesh, the unsprung leaves
Wound in the shells where silences are old,
Unarteried and green; where breathless rumours hold
Articulations of the mouthing sun,
Naming the colours countenancing cold of winter,
The fertile instances of sleep. And folded
Upon these ruins and on the one
Wind of sufferance the faltering word ungrieves.

It turns in this, autumn's true pastoral,
Spring's benefice of flowers and winter's kindest cry,
Joined in blood's binding litany where sun
Broods in them all, breathing its lonely
Fires from their breath, even as frostfalls come,
Sealing the assembling moods of miracle,
Muffling spring's waning word and undertone,
Feathering the stones until their breath is dumb
And the fretful leaves call stars to wake upon their sky.

And I, who hold the same moods in my lover
And in my craft and innocence to call the endless light
Into a poem to outstay that shade
Arranging time's true falsehoods at her head,
Watching all green to gold and into crown,
Change with the changing word and hear the chaffinch
Hover soundless between the notes of light and blood,
And see to mark this mystery and crown
Aureoles at leaf and stone and candles to the night.

Doubts of Mary, Madonna

The tree's sap rises. There is no other prayer
So certain of answer or so sure
Of responding light. The true sun's fountains share
Earth with those back in earth. Who restless with care
Will wake them, call them again? Sire
Christ, for your tree be drawn towards your star.
She who is flesh will welcome you, rare
Son, is of the dead unborn, their flesh, their fare.
Madonna, know his mouth. His mortal breath
Nurtures his beat of an immortal heart,
Numbers the words of the tree, counts his own death,
The days that cut dark and the light apart.
Summoned from dark in hope for the hungry dead
The unborn child's green buds blaze in her head.

The unborn child's green buds blaze in her head,
Enclose her sleepless midnight with the four
Walls of his sudden rainbow's silk and fire;
Give answers to all questions in the one word
Of his birth. Her senses hang blinded
Until at her finger-ends she feels the flower
Of the world burn then sees his shade retire
In a white train of angels overhead.
Annunciation strikes from the long sun:
But she feels leaves curl under the frost
That spreads in human blood her altered vein
Will bear, the endless summer of his last
Cry, how in the frost, frost in the flower at sin,
His loud and lasting infancies begin.

His loud and lasting infancies begin
In the waters of Eden, in the bright
Myth of grace where dispensations of light
Fell on the bed of that doomed garden.
Whose poison in that tree? Adam and Eve ran
In the rain of whose anger? The guilt, the flight

Left the garden empty. It only meant
The serpent was left to eat its own tail again.
At this boy's tongue such thin-lipped litanies
As lasted rose again. They hang in air
Unsaid until he adds new syllables,
Sees new heavens in the old pits. Despair
Dies where he'll come to his own death with calm
Rejoicing branches and the trodden palm.

Rejoicing branches and the trodden palm
Hold him in paradox. Their long embrace
Through stiffening fingers reach at his mother's face
Coming through generations to his psalm
Whose bones took shape and shelter in her womb.
She bears him, royal burden. Ice
Would melt at his gaze, thunders release
Notes for his lullaby, the iron tomb
Give clean to the keys of his sleeping eyes.
But her heart, wise in fears, hears the sad hymns
Of the future threaten, the kingly cries
Of weather wound the season in his limbs.
She takes him out of grief before the swords
Cut off the changeless silver of his words.

Cut off the changeless silver of his words:
He tells my death, his own, in his brief flame
And prayer. The sacrament of his name
Affords the counted feathers of the birds
Unlikely and unlooked for crumbs, rewards
Beyond the thrust of the given charm
Of singing. The law was to fly from harm
As long as they flew; and nothing afterwards.
Now his flight in dark stays off the vesper dark,
His whispers persuade fall to father praise
On lips, my own, on solemn tongues to mark
His double birth in her time's languages
Whose doubt took seed in crossing fire and shade
Through the first word of heaven in her head.

Through the first word of heaven in her head
She hears the death of trees. They strike the green
Foliage and parables of the Nazarene.
His miracles curve through her drift of blood.
Here is the first recession of the word
From human walls since his silk rainbow's sign
Sowed her stunned flesh with the approaching grain
Of the blown world when death is harvested.
Hearing the incantation of the kiss
Telling him to the frost before his fruit
Can fall to coming cold, to all's last bliss
She feels an agony, a prophetic root
Start at the dead in dreams, the children wound
Where his prayer touches stone and nurtures ground.

Where his prayer touches stone and nurtures ground
With a torn tongue, she rises to the cry
In the hung heat of his eclipsing sigh.
Between the sun and night, in his dragged wound,
Her son hangs hollow. The blackened-towned
Cloud of his waking gospel burns in high
Morning. His river of life runs dry.
But sap runs in his word; his dust is sound.
Her churches topple in the sudden blast
Of his bone from breath, her breathing and her light,
Rafter and rib in single utterance, lost
By murder, nails, lust of the blind sight.
The tree's leaves riot, sharpen to thorns and hide
Deep as the sorrows in his wasted side.

Deep as the sorrows in his wasted side
His dazzling shadow slips to truth and she
Watches the writing branches of his tree
Inscribe his second daybreak in the wood.
Her tears prepare his never-buried shroud,
Cleanse his sweet wounds from sweat's salt perfidy.
In grief she approaches grace, faithfully

In flesh has power to make the brightening cloud
Divide for the ascension of her starry king.
His apparition in its song's ascent,
The naked note and sinew of his wing
Splinter the gate of doom's frail covenant.
Midsummer frosts assemble to atone
Where he is hidden in the hollow stone.

Where he is hidden in the hollow stone
He rises, found. The shell lets out its light
Into the corners of her coming day, her rightful
Resurrection. So though she weep and mourn
His passing from the short days of the sun
The tree continues and she knows the might
Of her waiting children at its root
Bud in its stillness, poise, uncoil and burn.
Madonna, with hindsight see the arrayed
Promises and vestments come from a star
Beyond explanation. Its light has strayed
Into the pathways of the buried ear.
Children, when lost, weep; and they weep in fear.
The tree's sap rises. There is no other prayer.

Sonnet for his Daughter

Flesh her flesh spun, eyelid and hand and hair,
Crumb out of corn that spun her in her time,
Her mother before her, princes in a tomb
And mountain, Ophelia in the river,
My heartbeat sentinels, stalks across your blood.
And so, my midnight listener, wild owl call
Blind for carrion, with the long dead fall
Unravelling leaves, haunts the October wood.
Ghosts shade about your head. But invisible
Horses fly in the air and mark you down
For their calm kingdom. Mountain and water run
Under their hooves. Indestructible
Bird-notes, their spell, tangle within your skull,
And knot your story, make my soon death full.

Midwinternight

Midnight chimes at the locks
And the wind wrangles and tangles
The strokes of the country clocks
At the door of the room
Where my child lies calm,
Transfixed in sleep beside her mother.
Under her gentle arm
As sure as silence she shelters
And dreams though the loud dark groans
In the winter of rain and ruin and drums
That thump out tunes with the air's mad bugles.
Still the child sleeps though the village
Rocks on its hinges
And the weathercock changes
His strut every second and screaming
And striding to last on his spiral perch,
That the rain rusts, he spins for a star
That will herald him peace as the gale racks
His heart and the yew breaks.
But she dreams on nothing, and nothing
Will make her stir or cry
From her land of the delicate green trees
And the featherlight sun that stands warm
In her sleep and kind in its sanities.

Her midnight tolls in the flowers and tells
(In a country of descants of harebells
That more than her quiet breath buffets,
Her slightest sigh ruffles and rules)
That the gales cannot charge
Through her eyes with their dirge
And the rain cannot bullet her dream with its rifles.
Yet slowly, slowly, without her murmur or cry
The secret weather that works in to-night
As in all nights and summer, ever and ever,
In her heart though she sleep,

In day though she walk in remotest laughter,
The time that is always with her
Waits for her eyes to awake and raise up
The sun that is kind from its dark;
For her breath, though she die,
To calm the mad strokes of the wind into sleep
And the whole world turn as in blindness
To the green of her far-off trees that grow
To be struck into nearby blossom
And the flower of the carefree country she
By her glance and the children of sleep knows well
As grains of the sand know sea.
So in the country she dwells in she sleeps
And the wind as it is is as nothing,
The clocks out of year and the timed waves
Chiming in air as the still air keeps
Still thunder of graves and wintertime.

Homage to a Folk-Singer

Phil Tanner, born 1862

This evening is colder, but sit here by the hedge
The first leaves fallen on fire at your feet.
That thrush knows that cold will come. The stones
On the downs will not warm in the sun
Again this summer. This season, autumn, this silence,
Singer, is yours, for an old tune out of the sea.

Turn your face to the channel. Gaze past the headland
Where in the rock silence breeds secret wishes,
Death seeds itself in stone and, set to mark birds down
And their notes, would lock the charmed sea out.

In air and sea bells strike and death runs back
To sleep in the river-bed, the cliff-face:
So silence keeps its place, fixed with a dead shot.

Late? It's too soon for sleep. Past times are up
With us to-night and shake their bells at our bones,
Bury in waves of ringing the step that could sound
On the stair, this, any winter, drown striking clocks
As under the sure frost the sure spring dreams.

Those bells are yours that wave the sea's waves up
To sing of shipwrecks in the bay
And gold that shines like the moon
That lights lovers, love in the green lane.

Do not sleep yet. The tune turns with the wind
For the white sprays of silks and flowers,
Decks dancing weddings, wassails and whistles, brings
Time from the century's grave and furrow, unstops
Old music; and silence, rock, frost, fire, must wait.

★　★　★

Rocks are arrayed, are worked with green
Of weeds that have no words, being of rock.
The sea in our sight is green nearly always;
For it is green at the spine
Of each wave, and fragile blues soon break
With weather. So true sea waters speak
From green for those who sailed or drowned
Down the deep main, whose eyes sea closed,
Salt found, sand settled round
To wind long strands and stories in their brain.

The silent grey of the rocks would prove
That shade outlasts all loves, all lands,
All pure colours of the prism.
But children will clap their hands
For the spring because of the green
That gladdens them at the window-pane
When old men have told them wisely,
"Yes, one more frost is due."
The children do not understand:
"What is the frost but silver?" they demand.
Green is the colour they best know
By dreams of prophecy,
Their careful sleep's experience
And emerald innocence.

They can afford to sleep, being young,
To feed on stuff later years lie about
Saying "Green fails". Black frost is on that tongue.
Age must hold out, keep waking when the eye
Would close its lid perfidiously,
Disprove the stony lie,
And tell of all green sounds that ever rang
When April sprang and girls were garlanding.
I hear them as you sing.

★   ★   ★

Now it is nearly dark. Before we go
Sing as the moon comes up
Of wassailing's white cup
And Henry Martin's story
Of robbing the salt sea, too long ago.

And sing of Fair Phoebe
In a silken gown
With her dark-eyed curly sailor
Whose glance for her was crown.
And for her cruel beauty
Sing, too, of Barbara Allen
Dead in Scarlet Town.

As the moon rises
Sing of the Green Bushes,
The Banks of Primeroses,
Of lovers arm in arm who are gone
To cold, yet who laugh immune
From cold in the long days of a tune.

Sing of every bride for whom
"Green trees the shaded doors did hide".
Bells would have clanged their iron thin
To keep their quiet bodies from the tomb,
From the deep grave, the hands of stone.
But they still ring for true love,
And those figures shall remain:

And look, in moonlight now
They walk with us.
Dancers, lovers, sailors kiss their brides.
O, they are gone now!
But listen, hear them cry
Where the long waves ride:
There, suddenly, hear them!
They sing with their hearts' green bells, merrily.

For his Son, Unborn

So his heart's truths begin
In golden genesis
Roused by the eye's unfolding grain.
His pulse sets out to sing
Ghost of relentless origin.
Sounds of all human harvest
Net on his listening skin,
Keep covenant at his waking
In love's full lofts,
Dark treasuries and shafts,
Cut at his nine months' making.

He grows on the breath in night
With darkness about a star
Shining, unburning bright
On the retreating, turning waves
Of moondrawn tideless loves.
Words at his silent tongue
Voice secrets of the riding drowned
Waves of the sharp sea kiss
Then send to saltless ground.
Yet at his lips are hung
Secrets of light
Only the flying birds relate,
How the sun's songs are sung.

October names his limbs.
Its stalks and roots advance
To break his silences with dreams,
And starlight-slowly, gently coil
Its visions in his sleeping skull
And his beginning blood.

May-twig blossoms re-invade
Each vein and figured artery,
Dressed in all-mothering shade.
Hidden, midnight-river moved
In innocence and doom, he lies
With wisdom-wound and gloried eyes
Set on the first glad emerald,

And his heart's histories
Rise from the proffering dark
Of holy estuaries
Though his burning birth be dumb
His early furies fall to snow;
Though no high words
Can stay the falling spades
The settling ash and drifting spark,
Endless air and telling lark
Bearing blessings to his lids.

My Dusty Kinsfolk

My dusty kinsfolk in the hill
Screwed up in elm, when you were dead
We tucked you though your hands were still
In the best blanket from your bed
As though you dozed and might in stirring
Push off some light shroud you were wearing.

We did it against the double cold,
Cold of your deaths and our own.
We placed you where a vein of coal
Can still be seen when graves are open.
The Dunvant seam spreads fingers in
The churchyard under Penybryn.

And so you lie, my fellow villagers,
In ones and twos and families,
Dead behind Ebenezer. Jamjars
Carry flowers for you, but the trees
Put down their roots to you as surely as
Your breath was not, and was, and was.

Early and lately dead, each one
Of you haunts me. Continue
To tenant the air where I walk in the sun
Beyond the shadow of yew.
I speak these words to you, my kin
And friends, in requiem and celebration.

At his Father's Grave

Here lies a shoemaker whose knife and hammer
Fell idle at the height of summer,
Who was not missed so much as when the rain
Of winter brought him back to mind again.

He was no preacher but his working text
Was *See all dry this winter and the next.*
Stand still. Remember his two hands, his laugh,
His craftsmanship. They are his epitaph.

City in Fire and Snow

If those who stand so steadfastly beyond
The grave beckoned, how should we answer?
From cold that never ceases
To be original cold the long slow tides
Of summer cannot keep me.
                    For into every particle
Of flesh an ancient winter rides,
Hangs heavy on my eyelids, intrudes
Its certain ghost. Cold comes to its own kind.
I die by new natural wound
Though one signed my heart with blood,
Silenced for ever death in the winter wood.

Angelus bells for ritual frost begin
Their clear call for service.
In fear I contrive my fire.

I

Snow in the city. The girl dreamed
Deep of her death. Ordained and anaesthetic
Whiteness wore at her true world;
Midnight lay in cold for time to go out.

In pits of sleep she heard her first
Cry and her last echo across ice.
White catafalques, from glacial hills
Above her, fell whipcrack to the sea.
Between her first cry and her last
A mute, primeval spring's
Music of the impossible.

She dreamed; and sleeping down
To landscapes of lean valleys met
Rearing eyeless horses whinnying
Pricked by frost on the flanks to pound
To nowhere save her midnight.
She fell fast in sleep and fell
Under their hoofs to her own dark
Under my hands; in the end of her blood
Lay still for the hands of death
In winter half in welcome.

In her season of sleep by the struck sea
Waves in the roll and coil of breaking
Hung caught at the pinioning cold of the air.
The city and the fate that took it,
The snow of the flesh and fire were lost to her.
Though she breathed at my side my lover left me
In my land that suddenly out of a cloud
Wore flame, a scarlet shroud
Over the cold in every cell of the town:
At every corner, animals of fear.

She in her dreaming country saw
The blind, the groping snow
Accept the imperfect world, bestow
Spectre and final grace on all.
Wood, field, wave, broken wall.
She could not wish to leave
The scurried-clean unquestioning cold of her end,
Full winter's winding sheet,
Her death, her dignity's regalia.

But she woke to the snow of the flesh,
The hissing snow
On the lips of the last fires.
She rose from where alone
In the corner of her dream her heart
Lay without hope for other than the snow,
Seeing the heart of the sun in ice,
Her orient the silver coralled bowers
And cowls of the frozen sea.

Sleep now and rest. Lie where the light
Of the snow will take you and hold you fast.
Lie with me now for the snow lest fire part us.
Love, in your heart lie still. The cold is ours
And fire shall not touch us.
This my love said on the tip of doom.

Who was she then who was mine?
A price in her brain possessed her
Utterly beyond me and the arches of the fire
In the dream that took her bone.

How could I then persuade
This stranger of my bed
To journey with me, pay out the silk of breath
Through shifting labyrinths,
The walls of Sodom and Gomorrah
When salt and snow were all her sight
And whitest death the shape and trade of her word,
And wishing no escape?

And love do not turn from my side
And that which must be soon or late
For our love or sins, our summer or our hate.
Our sins burn here in the flames,
Are near in the town, in the snow
Whose next hands will be kind to us.
Let the fire pass, wait for the after-snow.
She touched my arm with a kiss.

Who was she then who was mine? Her land extended
Under fire's kingdom, under the ending town,
And she would lead into frost
My blood with her own in its winter fall,
Her world out of present winter,
The hands of the fire and my sun,
As I would hold her hard and away
For my love from her despair,
Knowing one way, the only way

From the near fire, the snow in the distant air,
The skilful fingers of disaster,
The way back far from the end of the town.

Racked on her kiss I knew her ghost
Founder to be alone from flesh,
That being too much set with harm
And always on its fires,
The weather of the world transmuted
To death on her tongue, the fruit sure.
For her the snow of my city
Whispered the snow beyond,
With love gone to the long shire
And in her night
Numbness became delight.

Held on her human kiss,
Alone to inhabit death I knew
Midnight take her certainly
For the town's doom beyond my words and grief,
The innumerable moments of her body
Left at this instant against silence,
The phantom horses' omnipresence,
The leaden leaf
Fall down and far forever,
Each bird die down,
And flight upon flight under the sheer hill
Snow's care arrange her, white on her white limbs,
Alone to inhabit death.

I will wait for the fire to call the cold,
Stay with me still.

Thus was my lover dead while her blood
Ran true in her veins. Her brain
Was chained in the waves of endless snow.
She could not come to the safe caves
In the hills of escape
Where sin was a story and the world could begin again.

She would kiss death, put off her robes
And lie under death's sharp ribs.
For in my land
Fire was the peacemaker,
Red fire was omega.

II

Whisperer of death, O whisperer
Two streams run in the heart.
One falls oblivious in a cataract
White with fear yet hurtling down
Drawn by it knows not what.
The other would flow calm
Away from snow and hurt
Whisperer, O whisperer.

Whisperer, O whisperer
She whom I love is gone
And dares to face death's weather slow or soon
Without a thought of pain
Yet would not die alone.
Whose work now to remain
In the whirlwind blast of the new sun
Whisperer, O whisperer?

Whisperer, what right to know
The hour of the second snow
When foliage may wave green
Under the beckoning horizon?

From the ancient mountaintops
The rivers still cascade,
Shapes from high hill sources
Sharing earth's first voices,
Into the divided valleys, on they ride.
Ice marks victory
On water with an easy blade;
Can the evil sun burn dry

And stifle all with a bright shade
In once, O deafening lips?

O word of death in the ear
Will she die easily
Since she would die and will not come away?
Or will the poisonous fire
Linger her from the day
She waits and wishes for,
Sear her with hell's alchemy
Whisperer, O whisperer?

Whisperer, what right to rest
In terrible beds of fire or frost
When lovers may lie close
Away from terror's house?

O shall she suffer death
With blood stopped suddenly
Or will long cancers endlessly
Scald her in every limb,
Blind her, prolong the long wails of the sky,
Withhold her deepest dream, allow no way
To turn it to desired mortality
Away from strangling breath?

O ghostly murmurer,
Wraith mouthing, *Kill her*,
How shall she die,
Whisperer, O whisperer?

III

As she lay in her cell of flesh with her dear vision
The walls inscribed unalterably with frost
Broke stone from stone, let in the slow
Snow-covered creepers waiting without,
Tendrils and stalks with waxen leaves
To decorate her shoulders.
She lay alone, alas, and kept from me.

She half-arose and tenderly
Plucked a silver berry from
The dark stem of a winding tree,
Put it to her faithless lips,
Tasted its bitterness with her teeth,
Smiled as if it were sweet
Fruit taken red in a gentle garden.
She half-arose and said:

The world is far at the end.
Who walks with us as we loiter and wait
For fingers to close on the shoulder
And turn us towards the last way?

Those around us crowd about,
A screen between us and ourselves
But one figure comes through their ranks,
Unseen and silent, leading their long way.

At whose hand did we take the path
Through the tangles of the false wood
With snow in the heart ever nearer,
Its country growing about the heart?
I eat the cold fruit of all – alone.
I have come to the centre of the forest,
To the tall, last tree
Before the world and fire are far.
I come upon a still and perfect scene.
White is the true green.

This death was her desire,
Her chosen end her gesture,
Her final wish in the snow
To take her to snow, her final breath
Kept for confession. My love sought sleep
Naked in winter's catacombs.

The girl went to the window, watched the night
Winding, the slack sails of the fall

Now hanging down, now caught and bellied up
By a gust, now curtained all together;
Now ripped in streamers, torn
In the midnight that might be noon.
Then she went down, walked slowly to the garden
And saw the near sky pour fire like rain.
So soon, she said, and *Soon*, she said again.

I followed her and kissed her,
Put my hands about her throat,
Gently upon my lover who had gone
Down to remotest lands,
Whose senses stayed in this;
And at my kiss
I pressed my fingers tight.
Her end came soon.

Out of the skies
A fluster of wild white flakes
Flecked at my eyes,
Intricate eddies and whirls
Of winter's afterblast.
The myth of her death
Was her dream and a world away.

IV

Green sleep, do not let this snow touch her
Nor cold mark the carnation of her flesh;
Nor let the envious fire
Disturb or finger her. Still in her cell of stillness
Yet let her sleep though the snow cry,
The bled air thunder, the bleeding stars wheel near
In riot, clap up the seas to sing
With drums in every crest.
This death was her desire,
Her death her expiation and
Her agony her rest. This my fingers have despoiled,
This naked child,
But, whisperer, she did not burn.

V

By the city, the mask of the city in snow,
By the city in fire, the city split in two,
Between the elements,
Between the snow and the fire I went,
Between her midnight and my own;
Where the town was taken and destroyed
And where the town still stood
In corridors of two ways of light
In streets where the red world met the white
I walked away from her death in the middle grove
Between my fear and my love.

Here buildings flowered red upon the air
And here a street, inaccurate and pale,
Lit but unconquered by the flame;
And here the fire burst tall
And there the snow furred on a wall;
Between two seasons of the soul,
One in its roaring end, the other asleep and slow,
I walked and watched the terror leap
But fail to destroy the further snow.

And as I turned to the only way to the sea
I passed where fire had had its way
And saw such faceless figures stalk,
The lost in blood, the torn, the terrible walkers
Seeking impossible safety blindly
Lost in the heart of the fire's fringe;

And from them stepped unscathed and strange,
One man living among the living dead;
And there he followed me,
There where I fell, he leapt, moved easily.

I waited for him. Here was one, I thought,
Who knew this part of what had been the city
Well, and would lead me

By some passageway underground.
But when I stopped and signed
To call him to come on
There as a roof and a wall tumbled red
Petals of fire like a rose,
Motionless he stayed under it, and did not move
Until I moved again, and then he followed on:

Through the arcaded gardens of inferno,
The narrow avenues, the mazes
Peopled by dead,
Their arms outstretched to embrace the fire,
The dead struck kneeling in homage
At the cry, the words of the giver of peace,
The dead as in stone but moaning in their age,
The children dead where the windows fell
To the familiar street
As if they had gladly watched the snow
Then suddenly were wise,
The white dust of the world upon their eyes.

And once I saw his shape
Stoop where a child lay beautiful and dead,
A golden-headed girl. He touched her head,
Lifted her up and laid her where
Fire left an alcove.

Then he came on
But would not walk with me
Though I beckoned again
And he coming ever nearer
Pointed on still
Until I saw his meaning
– Safety in separation from each other
Under the buildings' fire-drunk leaning
And falling, the steel veins bending
And falling under the unending wind of fire
Scattering the sky's broad arch of blazing snow.

And when at the edge of the town
He came towards the sea
Again the vortex snow spun endlessly
Over the shore, puffed up and winnowed down,
White poplar leaves blown red
Away from the angry breath
But still in the dome of fire.
The shuttling threads of snow worked in the air
To a hanging pattern of blood.
I waited for him, but he had disappeared.

Glad then to be alone
I started on the arc of the bay
For at the end there lay
The inland road to the hills,
Until I saw him come
Walking the lit waves
Near the shore
With his limbs in flame
Leading three children,
Naked each one for the whip of spray.

As they came near I ran
And saw him leave them sink to drown
Washed by the tide and bloody foam.
He waded to the sands
Ahead of me, and with fiery hands held out
Waited to greet me.

This man I saw with the bright body,
Had darkness in the holes that were his eyes.

VI

Whose shape is fire, whose company is flame
Nurtured by frost? Who stands apart from the ranks
And names the next, ally and enemy
And deals them all the same mortality?
Ice or fire from the sea,
Snow or huge fire from the air, the young, the old,

All, all are held,
Immensely walled or casually felled
By his finger and wasted by his eye:
He who unbridles hosts
Of his milkwhite horses, mounts for the weary ghosts
Worn out by his gaze, who gently
Lifts up the withered, loads the light mariner,
Whose dark beneath his brow
Swallows the bird from its climbing days
And the green flying prow
To lay them deep and down
As his choice as bride; embellishes
Wreaths in the vaults, his marriage chambers;
Would chastise even the sun
With his particular heat,
Would hold the golden coin in coffins
And speculate on blood with such deceit
As buys the world with his dark mineral.

Half turned away he took his cloak
Of fire slashed with brighter fire,
Embroideries with smouldering stones.
Throwing it off into the wind
He bared his bidding breast.
There flames in snakesheads twined and lay
Flicking their tongues; at either wrist
Red spluttering ruffs of fire.

He raised his hands to stroke
The smoothness of the cheek
I had thought in the town was lit
By the hysteric ruins and holocaust.

There where he stood the humbled realm of the tide
With tumbling walls in torn vermilion,
Creepered and wealed and wild,
Threw down its raging, wreathed,
Tendrilled and scalloped fields,
Liquid cornelian,
Threw up its dead white fish,

Calm seabirds white and dead
Ensnared and caged by snow;
Birds bound in branched weeds from the deep
Water that never saw the light
Until to the rattle of pebble and bone
It washed at red shingle and at his feet.

Then his voice as a voice in a shell,
The voice that said, *Be still.*

VII

With that reluctance in his walk
That keeps a lover gently back
From reaching O too soon his love,
Each movement savouring the fine
Threads of impeding air between
The other and the one,
He moved towards me, vacant eyes
Fixing me in the wilderness
That would be death. The elaborate waste
And wonder of the weather, the lost
Country and cry of the turned world
Was buried beneath the hill:
Again the whispered words, the words *Be still.*

He took me by the arm
And led me. Slowly the way I had planned
I walked, but with him.
And as we walked the ranges of the snow
Fell down before him. We went
With the storm moody and limping out
Until it was spent
Where his arm led the way.

Death brought me to her in the hills
And we were one again where I had gone;
I saw him come where the fury
Of fire was nothing, and slow ice nothing,
The town gone and, below, the silver country.

VIII

She stood with the wings of the cold
Spread over her, the air antlered
And hung with the lights of his long
Love stars, each nailed in its own north.
She moved as he approached, knelt down

And then in silence
Lay to lie for me and his love,
Postured and praising in the white
Roses of winter's enormous bridals
Of the children of the ghost
And the frost of spent stars.

A snap of his fingers kindled snow candles
At the corners of the love-bed of dust.
He hailed with his hand as she smiled.
Then he turned again and was easily
Scaling the hills and was gone.

She said: *In your heart lie still,*
My love, the cold is ours.
The fire cannot touch us.
Do not turn from your bride
In dark's new generations.

She moved, and found me. Below,
Between the hills and the emptying sea's
Homage, lay the city in fire and snow.

II

SATURDAY PICTURES

Daffodil in Snow

Among the stars inhabiting the snow
Steadfastly one slow sun evolves its glow.
Green flames, then yellow, then a surer gold
Sway down the silver distances of cold.
Here, in a while, the galaxy will dwindle
To nothing and its melting death rekindle
New fire from dark to set the sun at once
Ablaze upon its new impermanence.

Gulls

Startled and startling whiteness. White of wing
As white of snow above the morning tide.
Whiteness as white of waves just toppling:
White crest, white feather, shaded underside.

The war of flight. Neutrality's restraint
From early sunlight mustering new brightness.
Instant of new possession, new complaint.
Instant of whiteness overtaking whiteness.

Sow under an Oak

On Circe's swinish island long ago
Mariners charmed from manhood into beasts
Wandered the groves and, snouting to and fro,
Grunted their curses at remembered feasts.

But this Arcadian goddess is content
With what she finds within her Happy Valley,
Follows her whim, finds life is provident,
And not a human pang disturbs her belly.

Lovers in a Landscape

Inside their ornamental maze
Of days and wishes, signs and sighs,
An old design directs their ways:
Each path leads to the other's eyes.
The maze extends its walls to cover
Separate patterns of the past.

They have no threads to rediscover
The gates they entered to be lost:
And moving in the same elision
From what they knew to new illusion
They shape a common redivision
Of old designs from new confusion.

Mirror

A peeling mirror at an auction sale
A gazing girl, together tell a tale
That springs from more than casual connection:
It is the imperfection of reflection.

All glass is false. What image does not twist
Beauty the wrong way round? So truth is missed.
Yet Beauty, bidding against Isolation,
Will take the second-best, approximation.

A Chimp Gazes at his Hand

If you're the kind that simply can't endure
The moment when a secret seems to slip
Just out of reach you feel you can't be sure
Of knowledge though it's on your finger-tip.

So though you're always seeking the solution
To problems of heredity you doubt
(Even when face to face with evolution)
that soon you'll grasp just what it's all about.

Sonnet for Satchmo

Secular Gabriel, trumpeter who can put
Blues-time St. Vitus dance in any foot,
Wait for the casually integrated flounce
Of drums, trombone, piano. Then announce
Above the tapped accordances of feet
That Satchmo swings again down Basin Street.
Flex out the muscled notes and so convulse
To your own tempo the most glacial pulse;
Fingers, witch-hazelled lips, and lungs possessed
By dark agilities. Now, twelve bars rest.
And, after the magnetic pause, resettle
Your careful mouth against compulsive metal
To armstrong music out and to infer
A common rhythm's rarity. Yes, sir.

Cuckoo in the Nest

An old complaint. The owner-occupier
Tending, like many another, to aspire
To more than what she was, was quite impressed
And ready to accept that in her nest
An extra egg appeared; and, in delusion,
Hatched it among her own. Here's the conclusion.

By that possessive logic, with the quirk
Of nature that can put conceit to work
Where laziness will not, a cuckoo grows
Fat on the kind of care that never knows
That, given the proper quarter, one can be
Fed well on love that's laced with vanity.

Father nursing Boy

When at last he returned from that too long journey
They told him the child had been born, that his wife was dead.
And then every morning for months he climbed to the stony
Cemetery path, her forgiving voice in his head.

Some chided the length of his grief, but in gentler tones
Than they had used when once they had spoken his name.
And still he sat by the wall in the long afternoons
As months became years, and still his remorse was the same.

Doe and Suckling Fawn

Down in Debussy's forest something stirs.
Two animals are running round the trees.
One is all fun, the other one all ears.
One is adroit, one weaker at the knees.

The wobbly one gets tired. This explains
Why playtime ends so quickly, why so soon
Refreshment's needed. The interlude remains
The high-spot of a small fawn's afternoon.

III

✳ ✳ ✳ Cathedral Builders

They climbed on sketchy ladders towards God,
With winch and pulley hoisted hewn rock into heaven,
Inhabited sky with hammers, defied gravity,
Deified stone, took up God's house to meet Him,

And came down to their suppers and small beer;
Every night slept, lay with their smelly wives,
Quarrelled and cuffed the children, lied,
Spat, sang, were happy or unhappy,

And every day took to the ladders again;
Impeded the rights of way of another summer's
Swallows, grew greyer, shakier, became less inclined
To fix a neighbour's roof of a fine evening,

Saw naves sprout arches, clerestories soar,
Cursed the loud fancy glaziers for their luck,
Somehow escaped the plague, got rheumatism,
Decided it was time to give it up,

To leave the spire to others; stood in the crowd
Well back from the vestments at the consecration,
Envied the fat bishop his warm boots,
Cocked up a squint eye, and said, "I bloody did that".

Design for a Tomb

Dwell in this stone who once was tenant of flesh.
Alas, lady, the phantasmagoria is over,
Your smile must come to terms with dark for ever.

Carved emblems, puff-cheeked cherubs and full vines,
Buoy up your white memorial in the chapel,
Weightlessly over you who welcomed a little weight.

Lie unprotesting who often lay in the dark,
Once trembling switchback lady keep your stillness
Lest marble crack, ornate devices tumble.

Old melodies were loth to leave your limbs,
Love's deft reluctances where many murmured delight
Lost all their gay glissandi, grew thin and spare

Between a few faint notes. Your bright fever
Turned towards cold, echoed remembered sweets.
Those who for years easily climbed to your casement

Left by the bare front hall. Lust grown respectable
Waltzed slow knight's moves under the portico,
Crabbed in a black gown. You were carried out

Feet first, on your back, still, over the broad chequers.
So set up slender piers, maidenhair stone
Like green fern springing again between ivory oaks,

The four main pillars to your canopy;
And underneath it, up near the cornices
Let in small fenestrations to catch the light.

It still chinks, spy-holing the bent laurel
With worn footholds outside your bedroom window
Through which you'd hear an early gardener's hoe

Chivvy the small weeds on the gravel path
Only to turn dazedly back into your lover's arms,
Fumblingly to doze, calling the morning false.

Lady-lust so arrayed in ornamental bed,
Baring your teeth for the first apple of heaven,
Juices and sap still run. Sleep, well-remembered.

Instructions to Settlers

who arrived in Patagonia from Wales, 1865

On these lean shelves of land
Nothing but thorn thrives.
At noon cross-winds foregather
To suck and subdivide
The dust and the white sand
Between one shelf and another.
With thornstumps then mark out
The plots for your bent lives.
This place is home. Possess
The wilderness with yourselves.
Dig deep. Cut down to zero,
Cut through land's wasted face
To where springs bitter with brine
Pulse sidelong and in vain
Under the restless dust,
Under the windworn plain;
And through the coarsest thorn
Strike with sharp dream, sharp bone
To reach brief union
With this mistaken Canaan.
Search here where seed was lost,
Work stone and white to green.
Ease your tormented ghost.

Message in a Bottle

for Val Howells

Mariner, the persuasion of the sea
Has worked its sleight of hand again,
Again the horizon's false. So far
Your luck's held out. The sun's come up
Roughly where you expected, has swung
Clockwise in the northern hemisphere.
So far you've kept fair bearings.

But what if I say that suddenly
Beyond that horizon and its horizon too
There is no more land, that after you put out
The meridian altered, all continents fell
Away, sucked down without a blink
Of light or sigh or semaphore?
Suppose I said, "Go sail the seas for an island,
There is none? No reef and no white water
Over coral; nothing but water, that is all your earth?"
That all your change of rigging, the fine
Rejigs to jib, genoa, spinnaker
Are vain, that all you do with the tiller
Will bring you back to nothing,
That even your departure jetty's gone,
That a slow stillness, ghost of a garden's
Fallen upon the lurching of your sea?

You'd shoot the sun again, compose yourself
With old assumptions, trust old courses
On interim charts, find reasons for the silence
On the radio, check your batteries,
Ignore the sinister becalment threatening
Your brain, curse everything before you took
New credence, believe anything rather than believe

Reality had changed, whatever reality is.
Be reassured, I'm talking to myself
And expect no-one to believe me.
But it would be madness to presume
The shore you reach will not be that of a desert,
And madness, too, to suppose that the white dust there
Will not canopy into roses and then yield wheat.

First Sleep

A threat of April in the seed
Drew me from nothing on a string.
My husk began in a caged harvest,
A river remembered light through ferns and leaves
Set in stones by ancient summers.
Through stone I heard the far sea cry
And grew away from dead dreamers.

Last autumn's stalks explored my limbs,
Their picks drew nearer my tomb,
Breaking my sleep, tapping my wall of skull.
I came alive in a familiar stall
Where night drew gold from the living hill.

Daybreak, daydream met on the moon's bright wires
Across the heads of that year's daffodils.
Dusk and eventless sleep withdrew their hands
Into the earth. Shaping the changeless clay
Their fingers feared the withering day.

From the arms of the mountain's ancestry
I moved to men with ancient eyes
Whose bones lay down with the bones of tragedy,
Whose lips knew words of the singing flood:
The river slept at my waking to the world.

Upstairs in this stone house,
Up the twelve crooked stairs
My mother climbed to bear me.
At eleven o'clock on a spring night
I fell from her dark into candlelight,
Came to my own flesh as the string was cut
And lay alone on the bloody sheet.

Poem in February

Upon a lank sea-shore in February
(Grave curl and cry of a whirlpool bay)
My footprints set a line to mark
That once my kin lived in the rock.
Here at dunes where the tides run back
Taliesin found his sanctuary.
Here nothing is destroyed but all things made
To be unmade are re-made again,
The geometry of tides continually engraved
On every counted sandgrain's head.

So when the winds through the marsh reeds
Cut from the channel to seek me out
My hair is sea-grass, fingers sand.
Over the arcs of water and the marks
Of footprints sprung from the seeds
Of rock they pass through nothing
And history, and find me as the land.

Where the thin sun combs out the greyhair cloud,
Drops an insistent shadow on the distant castle,
Broken like bone, there on the wall the skull's
No alien. And the black woods around
Witness no burial of the dead in the young seas
Or living committed under the castle mound.

Here I am not alone. For under all,
Under the leafmould and under the sea-wrack's
Palimpsest written by tide upon tide
The skull and I are one. The ebb and flow
Of the sun unlocks and wakes
Every spring suddenly, and one by one
They flood to this place and to now,
This endless February when first the primrose breaks.

Finding a Fossil

Maidenhair fern in flint;
An ancient accident
Shows me time's imprint.

A leaf preserved and pressed
Between leaves of stone; crossed
Rest and unrest.

An image that grew green
Took ground in the rock grain:
Dark; now light again.

Luck interlaced each line
And dying vein with stone.
They return to the same sun.

The casual life of fronds,
Air and the tongues of friends;
Green begins, grey ends;

Except that remembered shapes
Live, and that at one's lips
Love speaks as loves lapse.

Graftings (so fused in chance
Among cold stars that dance
Gestures of permanence)

Persist and contrive to invent
From fragment and element
A mindful firmament.

Three Rs

Lover, look in her eyes and heed
Reassurance, gentle signs;
But gazing long there do not read
Too deep between the lines.
Rather take care that you inscribe
In her soft palm with your slow fingertip
Such words as the unminding globe
Allow you still to hope;
So that your easy lessons make
Some mockery of the falling sun,
Your brief and charmed arithmetic
Prove, for a time, that one and one is one.

Tombstones

Inscriptions, ritual statements
Of time's imbalance, of resources
Drained from the bank of seasons,
Painfully tell us nothing. In due course
The stonemason's phraseology will tap
Its short syllables into the skull.

Could you spell out
At death's precise dictation
A three-line version of your own life?
Could you say more in less
At half-a-crown a cut letter?

Lichens censor all but the primitive
Incisions of arbitrary dates.
Ochre elisions, encrustations
Blur the clean granite lines
Of most lives set down here.

Epitaph for Uncle Johnnie

Here lies a tenor. For his grace rejoice.
His soaring notes rang out, the rafters rang.
He gave God glory with his golden voice
And lived the silver music that he sang.

After a Death

Come back to the house, I turn the key in the door,
Pull back the curtains to let out the dark,
Kindle a fire, wind up my grandfather's clock,
Then see the slug's trail on the kitchen floor.

I have inherited him with all the rest
Of whatever's here, the pictures, the jugs, the beds
Nobody sleeps in any more. Presumably he feeds
On something here. He wouldn't come for dust.

The tables and chairs are mine, the brass trinket box,
White plates that write their O's across the dresser,
The coats and shoes in cupboards, the old letters,
The pots, the pans, the towels, the knives and forks,

The small effects of other people's lives,
– And him who wasn't mentioned in the will
Who entered from the garden once and still
From time to time inspects his territory then leaves.

A list's a list and offers me no order,
I see the silver trail, know other presences.
A death's a death. I mourn three absences.
If I wait here they'll speak when time is older.

My Grandfather and his Apple Tree

Life sometimes held such sweetness for him
As to engender guilt. From the night vein he'd come,
From working in water wrestling the coal,
Up the pit slant. Every morning hit him
Like a journey of trams between the eyes;
A wild and drinking farmboy sobered by love
Of a miller's daughter and a whitewashed cottage
Suddenly to pay rent for. So he'd left the farm
For dark under the fields six days a week
With mandrel and shovel and different stalls.
All light was beckoning Soon his hands
Untangled a brown garden into neat greens.

There was an apple tree he limed, made sturdy;
The fruit was sweet and crisp upon the tongue
Until it budded temptation in his mouth.
Now he had given up whistling on Sundays,
Attended prayer-meetings, added a concordance
To his wedding Bible and ten children
To the village population. He nudged the line,
Clean-pinafored and collared, glazed with soap,
Every seventh day of rest in Ebenezer;
Shaved on a Saturday night to escape the devil.

The sweetness of the apples worried him.
He took a branch of cooker from a neighbour
When he became a deacon, wanting
The best of both his worlds. Clay from the colliery
He thumbed about the bole one afternoon
Grafting the sour to sweetness, bound up
The bleeding white of junction with broad strips
Of working flannel-shirt and belly-bands
To join the two in union. For a time
After the wound healed the sweetness held,
The balance tilted towards an old delight.

But in the time that I remember him
(His wife had long since died, I never saw her)
The sour half took over. Every single apple
Grew – across twenty Augusts – bitter as wormwood.
He'd sit under the box tree, his pink gums
(Between the white moustache and goatee beard)
Grinding thin slices that his jack-knife cut,
Sucking for sweetness vainly. It had gone,
Gone. I heard him mutter
Quiet Welsh oaths as he spat the gall-juice
Into the seeding onion-bed, watched him toss
The big core into the spreading nettles.

January Journey

The bus crosses New Brunswick
In expected snow; but nothing of ballroom glitter
With God the haut-couturier
Putting the long white evening-gloves on trees
And all arms raised in waiting
For the first note of the world's great waltz.
Here, snow the annihilator.

Though not to start. Uphill from Fredericton
Mounting intensity of whiteness. Doily scallops
On eaves and pastel shades of balconies discarded,
Pittsburgh-loud paints wiped out and nullified.
Drift-railings fuzz into nonentity.

League after league the non-scenic route
Of the blank world opens, mutates
Whiteness a thousand times
With each mutation whiteness:
Though birches reject all versions save their own,
Pines and bush bent with perpetually
Beginning beginning snowfall.
Today it will snow all day.

Into St. John. The frozen luggage thumps
Onto the slab of street. Then the engine climbs
Ten miles upon its long saw-whine
Refusing to give a semitone to the hill.
And then it gives an octave. We take aboard
A mother and child into our shaking shelter:
Their parcels thaw then settle on the rack.

Do you like ketchup? (says the child to his madonna)
                    Not too much.
It's good. You put it on chips.
                    Is that so?

And hamburgers.
                    I must try some.
What's your last name?
                    Brown.
Katie Brown?
                    No, Catherine Brown.
My last name's Brown, too.

And then the crew-cut boy
Notices my strangely-foreign mane of long grey hair.
He sees it from the front.

Why do you have all that hair?
                    Some people are lucky.

Roaming around he soon finds, from behind,
The round bald patch, my arctic circle.
He explores it with his warm hand.

Why aren't you lucky here?

Then this young philosopher
Poses his lady the key question:

If they threw me in jail,
Do you love me so much
You'd come down and bail me out?

So past the square flat igloos
Of the Sandman Motel for the Best Sleep.
Always we move towards the final weather.
Afternoon ending atomises whiteness:
Here where the land yielded but part of its truth
One colour encloses the shrinking world.

But not before, in Pioneer Cemetery
(Penobsquis 1801), the names of INNIS,
GRAY and HAMILTON leap square
From headstones shaved smooth by the barber wind.

Whoever they were, or are,
Jesus, the names cry out,
Do you love me so much
If they threw me six feet under the snow
Would you come down and bail me out?

Did the answer ever come
To this edge of Albert County?

One colour encloses the world.
Bringing his share of it, his foam-form with him,
Another voyager (No longer believe it's land)
Bears to us news of the lost sphere,
Says to my neighbour

Did you know your cousin was dead?
                    Who?
Harry Burnett. I'm going down to see him now.

The gears grace-note down. From a huge distance
Suddenly on us a snowplough blinks
In orange, heliographs clearance.

D'you ever go down to Freddie's at all
Or over to West Side?
                    No, far as I go
Is out to the bingo game.

One darker colour encloses the whole world
For all the small towns' neon signalling
And single country windows flashing their dim morse.

Ed Waters lost his wife last Monday.
                    You don't say.
You don't know anything at all...
Ned's pretty bad. He lost his woman too.

                    Harry Burnett, you said.
                    Harry was too fat.

D'you ever hear from Hamer?
                    No.
He's in the money, ain't he? He never writes.

Who ever writes?
Sweet Jesus, those stones cried out,
Do you love me so much
If they threw me six feet under the great weather
Would you get me off Death Row?

Innis. Gray. Hamilton,
Mrs. Ed Waters and you Harry Burnett,
And Ned whoever you are or were
So soon to follow your lost woman,
I too can see the sign
Nearly obscured by snow at the junction of the roads.
YIELD, it says, YIELD.
We do. Though this time we go on,
Slowly, towards Halifax.

The Ambush

after Giovanni Bellini's 'The Assassination of St. Peter Martyr'

Ring of black trees, late winter afternoon.
How came this bishop here in the elaborate fish-scales
Of his gold surplice, weighed down, unable to run,
Unable to flee to anywhere in the precise
Enclosing landscape, across the fields to the town
Or into the formality of the far pink hills?
Into the ring of trees wade men with swords.

The mute vermilion sun burns on their blades,
Reveals the fine, explicit, complex branches
On the horizon, every black twig exact;
With its slow falling it levers the horizon up.
The bishop and his attendants drop to their knees.
A slow light snow begins its imprecision
In this particular copse. The saints incur their wounds.
White flowers spring from the ground.

Earlier, woodcutters worked upon this spot,
Now see the tree-stumps bleed
Onto the snow with vegetable compassion
As these martyrs fall and die to rebellious men
Who make the copse a thicket with their spears.

The bloody sun's struck down. The eastern moon comes up.
In the slow beginning snow the saints
Cry out. Dusk, the still afternoon
Surrounds their cries, stifles their blood's music,
Their praise of the unfinished God.

I am the bishop, I am the men with the swords.

Michaelangelo to Himself, 1550

Forget the Pope, the dead weight of the tomb;
Remember Tuscany and summer.
On hill, in hollow, vineyards yawn awake,
The green wine stretches its arms below Caprese.
Above black cypresses sunlight sucks the grape
And turns the corner of the sky to harvest.
The light is never still, the shade's alive.

Half the madonnas blessing Italy
Gaze into dead dark high upon the walls.
Half the annunciations, crucifixions,
Conceived in day are lost in the church's night
As though to re-witness were to be with the damned.
The church is blind. Only the painters saw them.
The act of making is the act of worship.

Remember the rough, imperfect, constant
Promises of stone. With stubborn chisel
Tenderly bite and ease veins from the marble,
Limbs from the solid block with the soft grain.
Restore, justify shapes in their rightful order.
Startle the light. Let light be thunderstruck
With one more breathing occupant of rock.

After Petrarch

Memories of my youth, my wasted days
Now wound me with regret. Mere mortal things
Enchanted me and chained me, though I had wings
To soar aloft and make men lift their eyes.
O you who witness all my darkest ways,
Invisible God, heaven's almighty king,
Give succour to my soul, frail, wandering
And empty. Come, fill me with your grace:

So that while life was restless as the sea
I'll die calm and in harbour; though I was in vain
I'll journey towards death with honesty.
I pray that in what few short hours remain
To me you'll help me to attain
My hope in you – this the sole hope for me.

To a Nun

after the 15th century Welsh

Please God, forsake your water and dry bread
And fling the bitter cress you eat aside.
Put by your rosary. In Mary's name
Leave chanting creeds to all those monks in Rome.
Spring is at work in woodlands bright with sun;
Springtime's not made for living like a nun.
Your faith, my fairest lady, your religion
Show but a single face of love's medallion.
Slip on this ring and this green gown, these laces;
The wood is furnitured with resting places.
Hide in the birch tree's shade – upon your knees
Murmur the mass of cuckoos, litanies
Of spring's green foliage. There's no sacrilege
If we find heaven here against the hedge.
Remember Ovid's book and Ovid's truth:
There's such a thing as having too much faith.
Let us discover the shapes, the earthly signs
Of our true selves, our souls, among the vines.
For surely God and all his saints above,
High in their other heaven, pardon love.

The Hall of Cynddylan

after the Welsh of Llywarch Hên: 9th Century

Cynddylan's hall is dark to-night,
No fire and no bed.
I weep alone, cannot be comforted.

Cynddylan's hall is all in dark to-night,
No fire, no candle-flame:
Whose love, but love of God, can keep me sane?

Cynddylan's hall is dark to-night,
No fire, no gleam of light.
Grief for Cynddylan leaves me desolate.

Cynddylan's hall, its roof is charred and dark,
Such sparkling company sheltered here.
Woe betide him whose whole lot is despair.

Cynddylan's hall, the face of beauty fallen,
He's in his grave who yesterday stood tall.
With him alive no stone fell from the wall.

Cynddylan's hall, forsaken then to-night,
So snatched from his possession.
Death take me so and show me some compassion.

Cynddylan's hall, no safety here to-night,
On Hytwyth's high expanse
No lord, no soldiery, no defence.

Cynddylan's hall is dark to-night,
No fire and no music.
My tears carve out their ravage on my cheeks.

Cynddylan's hall is dark to-night,
No fire, the company's all gone.
My tears tumble down upon its ruin.

Cynddylan's hall, to see it pierces me,
No fire, roof open to the sky:
My lord is dead and here, alive, am I.

Cynddylan's hall, burned to the very ground,
After such comradeship,
Elfan, Cynddylan, Caeawc, all asleep.

Cynddylan's hall, anguish is here to-night.
Once it was held in honour:
Dead are the men and girls who kept it so.

Cynddylan's hall, too much to bear to-night,
Its chieftain lost, O
Merciful God, what can I do?

Cynddylan's hall, the roof is charred and dark
Because the Englishry wreaked havoc on
The pastureland of Elfan and Cynddylan.

Cynddylan's hall is dark to-night,
I mourn Cyndrwynyn's line,
Cynon, Gwiawn and Gwyn.

Cynddylan's hall, my open wound,
After the bustle, all the mirth
I knew upon this hearth.

Landscape without Figures

Cynddylan's hall is dark to-night,
Says the Welsh bard from the days of bows and arrows;
The blood of kinsmen reddened some small rivers,
The singing fool left helpless as usual.

There'd been some battle or other
Fought in a bog, no doubt; as unromantic
And merciless as ever. But fine phrases
Took in charred stones and rafters,
Dead fires under chimneys, benches overturned,
Many men dead out in the dank country.

The old poets were good at this kind of thing;
A bit high-flown, but genuine enough;
Cooking the metre but seldom the reaction.
I know how they felt in the evening wasteland of Wales:
I come upon a farmhouse with old stones tumbling,
The roof fallen-in, nettles at every lintel
And empty cowsheds crumbling, an elder
Loaded with berries and nobody to pick them.
No sign of blood, only tins and broken bottles,
But once lived-in, and now no longer lived-in.

The hall of somebody who was is empty to-night.
But there was a man and his house. It might be said
The elder blossoms each year in token celebration.

Froga

Two yew trees sentried his black garden gate
And every summer Sunday night
He stood between them, a general
Of misery, inspecting them and
The bad joke of the world,

His uniform a black suit, mildew green;
His black velour hat verdigrised round the band
From his sweat at life's jaundice.
His eyebrows were black moustaches,
His moustache the prototype
Of all those worn by practitioners
In the old ambulance books
Where the patient's beyond repair,
But his eyes not evil, rather
The eyes of a dying seal in a bankrupt circus.

Only once did I hear him speak, to scare
Off a blackbird that sang in his yew-tree.
Behind his back we called him Froga,
Half frog, half ogre.

I heard say that they buried him in his suit;
They didn't think it would burn:
And that in his coffin, because they'd taken out
His teeth, he lay there smiling.

Johnny Randall

When the moon was full (my uncle said)
Lunatic Johnny Randall read
The Scriptures in the dead of night
Not in bed by candlelight
But in the field in the silver glow
Across the lane from Howells Row;
And not to himself but to the sheep
With the village barely fallen asleep
And colliers who'd worked two-till-ten
In no fit shape to shout "Amen"
Grumbled "The bugger's off again".

He'd dip in Chronicles and Kings,
Dig into Micah, Obadiah
Lamentations, Jeremiah,
Ezekiel, Daniel, on and on
Into the Song of Solomon:
A great insomniac heaven-sent
Digest of the Old Testament,
Faltering only in his loud
Recital when a pagan cloud
Darkened the Christian moon and bright
Star congregation of the night.

Then Johnny Randall in a vexed
Improvisation of the text
Would fill in with a few begats
Of Moabs and Jehoshaphats
(Windows banged shut like rifle-shots)
And Azels, Azrikans and all
The genealogy of Saul,
Till David's line put out new shoots
That never sprang from royal roots
And wombs long-barren issued at
The angel seed of Johnny's shouts.

When clouds veered off the moon's clean rim,
Another chapter. Then a hymn
To close the service. So he'd sing

In the big deeps and troughs of sin
No one lifts up my drowning head
Except my bridegroom Jesus Christ
Who on the Cross was crucified...

Then silence. Benediction: May
The Love of God and
The Fellowship of the Holy Spirit
Be with you always
Till the great white moon comes again.

Stillness. Until at last
Johnny would rouse himself
And take up collection from the cows.

Postcard from the Past

Among old bills in a cluttered drawer
I come upon it, wonder why I kept it.
In lese-majesty and love the stamp's
Stuck upside-down. The postmark re-endorses
The name of the resort. Children on rubber horses
Tame the hand-tinted sea. But there is no address

Except my own – an old one – naming a place
Where I am known no longer. Stock phrases
And news of old weather send me a dead greeting.
The final signature is indecipherable.
Nothing makes sense except the final X.

Definition of a Waterfall

Not stitched to air or water but to both
A veil hangs broken in concealing truth

And flies in vague exactitude, a dove
Born diving between rivers out of love

In drums' crescendo beat its waters grow
Conceding thunder's pianissimo

Transfixing ancient time and legend where
A future ghost streams in the present air:

From ledge to pool breakneck across rocks
Wild calm, calm chaos skein their paradox

So that excited poise is fiercely dressed
In a long instant's constant flow of rest,

So that this bridegroom and his bride in white
Parting together headlong reunite

Among her trailing braids. The inconstancy
Is reconciled to fall, falls and falls free

Elegy for a Butterfly

On the flitting face of things – and given
A proper pedestrian approach to heaven –

Two words ought to have been enough. He died.
So smile as you will at the impassioned excess

Indulged herein. Perhaps it is laughable.
As far as I know no comets shot at his coming;

There was the usual genteel smell
In Cathedral Road the night of his end.

But if butterflies count the next truth
Puts him grieved now in considerable

Flighty grace beyond the millennium
Of his expectation. The odd fact is that

The imagined world spun under him.

He became whatever it was he was
Briefly in a most elaborate fashion,

Living an intense spent
Moment. There seemed no sense

In his living at all. After all
The brontosaurus and the pterodactyl

Long ago went to ground and are (according
To the evidence before the court) extinct.

Salmon

first for, and now in memory of, Ceri Richards

The river sucks them home.
The lost past claims them.
   Beyond the headland
It gropes into the channel
Of the nameless sea.
   Off-shore they submit
To the cast, to the taste of it.
It releases them from salt,
Their thousand miles in odyssey
For spawning. It rehearsed their return
   From the beginning; now
   It clenches them like a fist.

The echo of once being here
Possesses and inclines them.
   Caught in the embrace
Of nothing that is not now,
Riding in with the tide-race
   Not by their care,
Not by any will they know,
They turn fast to the caress
Of their only course. Sea-hazards done,
They ache towards the one world
   From which their secret
   Sprang, perpetuate

More than themselves, the ritual
Claim of the river, pointed
   Towards rut, tracing
Their passion out. Weeping philosopher,
They reaffirm the world,
   The stars by which they ran,
Now this precise place holds them
Again. They reach the churning wall
Of the brute waterfall which shed

Them young from its cauldron pool.
A hundred times
They lunge and strike

Against the hurdles of the rock;
Though hammering water
Beats them back
Still their desire will not break.
They flourish, whip and kick,
Tensile for their truth's
Sake, give to the miracle
Of their treadmill leaping
The illusion of the natural.
The present in torrential flow
Nurtures it own
Long undertow:

They work it, strike and streak again,
Filaments in suspense.
The lost past shoots them
Into flight, out of their element,
In bright transilient sickle-blades
Of light; until upon
The instant's height of their inheritance
They chance in descant over the loud
Diapasons of flood, jack out of reach
And snatch of clawing water,
Stretch and soar
Into easy rapids

Beyond, into half-haven, jounce over
Shelves upstream; and know no question
But, pressed by their cold blood,
Glance through the known maze.
They unravel the thread to source
To die at their ancestry's
Last knot, knowing no question.

They meet under hazel trees,
Are chosen, and so mate. In shallows as
The stream slides clear yet shirred
    With broken surfaces where
    Stones trap the creamy stars

Of air, she scoops at gravel with fine
Thrust of her exact blind tail;
    At last her lust
Gapes in a gush on her stone nest
And his held, squanderous peak
    Shudders his final hunger
On her milk; seed laid on seed
In spunk of liquid silk.
So in exhausted saraband their slack
Convulsions wind and wend galactic
    Seed in seed, a found
    World without end.

The circle's set, proportion
Stands complete, and,
    Ready for death,
Haggard they hang in aftermath
Abundance, ripe for the world's
    Rich night, the spear.
Why does this fasting fish
So haunt me? Gautama, was it this
You saw from river-bank
At Uruvela? Was this
    Your glimpse
    Of holy law?

Organist

Sole village master of the yellowing manual,
And market gardener: his sense of perfect pitch
Took in the cracks between the keys.
He was equipped to hear the tiny discord struck
By any weed which innocently mistook
His garden for a place to grow in.

Five days a week John Owen dug and planted,
Potted and weeded, worried
About Saturday's price in Swansea Market
For his green co-productions with God.

Walking to town at dawn, five miles
With Mary Ann his wife fluting beside him
(She, as they said, would laugh at her own shadow)
With creaking baskets laden, he nearly deafened
Himself with the noise of his own boots.

Sabbath, inside the spade-sharp starch
Of his crippling collar, he husbanded
On the harmonium aged couplers
And celestes into a grave, reluctant
Order; took no heed in the hymns
Of the congregation trailing a phrase behind,
Being intent and lost in the absolute beat.

But, with the years, philosopher as he was,
A Benthamite of music, he set more store
By the greatest harmony of the greatest number.
When, pentecostal, guilts were flung away
Fortissimo from pinnacles of fervour,
When all were cleansed of sin in wild
Inaccurate crescendoes of Calvary,
Uncaring, born again, dazzled by diadems

In words of a Jerusalem beyond their lives,
The choristers would stray from the safe fold
Of the true notes. John Owen would transpose
By half a tone in the middle of the hymn
To disguise the collective error,
But sure of the keys of his own kingdom.

He lies long since in counterpoint
With a few stones of earth; is beyond any doubt
The one angel of the village cloud
Who sings from old notation;
The only gardener there whose cocked ear
Can discern the transgression, the trespass
Of a weed into the holy fields,
If there are weeds in heaven.

The Key

Its teeth worked doubtfully
At the worn wards of the lock,
Argued half-heartedly
With the lock's fixed dotage.
Between them they deferred decision.
One would persist, the other
Not relent. That lock and key
Were old when Linus Yale
Himself was born. Theirs
Was an ageless argument.

The key was as long as my hand,
The ring of it the size
Of a girl's bangle. The bit
Was inches square. A grandiose key
Fit for a castle, yet our terraced
House was two rooms up, two down;
Flung there by sullen pit-owners
In a spasm of petulance, discovering
That colliers could not live
On the bare Welsh mountain:

Like any other house in the domino
Row, except that our door
Was nearly always on the latch.
Most people just walked in, with
'Anybody home?' in greeting
To the kitchen. This room
Saw paths of generations cross;
This was the place to which we all came
Back to talk by the oven, on the white
Bench. This was the home patch.

And so, if we went out, we hid
The key – though the whole village
Knew where it was – under a stone
By the front door. We lifted up
The stone, deposited the key
Neatly into its own shape
In the damp earth. There, with liquid
Metal, we could have cast,
Using that master mould,
Another key, had we had need of it.

Sometimes we'd dip a sea-gull's
Feather in oil, corkscrew it,
Far into the keyhole to ease
The acrimony there. The feather, askew
In the lock, would spray black
Droplets of oil on the threshold
And dandruff of feather-barb.
The deep armoreal stiffness, tensed
Against us, stayed. We'd put away
The oil, scrub down the front step.

The others have gone for the long
Night away. The evidence of grass
Re-growing insists on it. This time
I come back to dispose of what there is.
The knack's still with me. I plunge home
The key's great stem, insinuate
Something that was myself between
The two old litigants. The key
Engages and the bolt gives to me
Some walls enclosing furniture.

IV

Ancient Monuments

for Alexander Thom

They bide their time off serpentine
Green lanes, in fields, with railings
Round them and black cows; tall, pocked
And pitted stones, grey, ochre-patched
With moss, lodgings for lost spirits.

Sometimes you have to ask their
Whereabouts. A bent figure, in a hamlet
Of three houses and a barn, will point
Towards the moor. You find them there,
Aloof lean markers, erect in mud.

Long Meg, Five Kings, Nine Maidens,
Twelve Apostles: with such familiar names
We make them part of ordinary lives.
On callow pasture-land
The Shearers and The Hurlers stand.

Sometimes they keep their privacy
In public places: nameless, slender slabs
Disguised as gate-posts in a hedge; and some,
For centuries on duty as scratching-posts,
Are screened by ponies on blank uplands.

Search out the farthest ones, slog on
Through bog, bracken, bramble: arrive
At short granite footings in a plan
Vaguely elliptical, alignments sunk
In turf strewn with sheep's droppings;

And wonder whether it was this shrunk place
The guide-book meant, or whether
Over the next ridge the real chamber,
Accurate by the stars, begins its secret
At once to those who find it.

Turn and look back. You'll see horizons
Much like the ones that they saw,
The tomb-builders, millenniums ago;
The channel scutched by rain, the same old
Sediment of dusk, winter returning.

Dolerite, porphyry, gabbro fired
At the earth's young heart: how those men
Handled them. Set on back-breaking
Geometry, the symmetries of solstice,
What they awaited we, too, still await.

Looking for something else, I came once
To a cromlech in a field of barley.
Whoever farmed that field had true
Priorities. He sowed good grain
To the tomb's doorstep. No path

Led to the ancient death. The capstone,
Set like a cauldron on three legs,
Was marooned by the swimming crop.
A gust and the cromlech floated,
Motionless at time's moorings.

Hissing dry sibilance, chafing
Loquacious thrust of seed
This way and that, in time and out
Of it, would have capsized
The tomb. It stayed becalmed.

The bearded foam, rummaged
By wind from the westerly sea-track,
Broke short not over it. Skirted
By squalls of that year's harvest,
That tomb belonged in that field.

The racing barley, erratically-bleached
Bronze, cross-hatched with gold
And yellow, did not stop short its tide
In deference. It was the barley's
World. Some monuments move.

Paraphrase for Edwin Arlington Robinson

It was Sod's Law and not the sun
That made things come unstuck for Icarus.

The same applies to all with a seeming head
For heights, a taste for the high wires,

Flatulent aerialists who burped
At the critical moment then fell akimbo

In a tattered arc, screaming, down
Out of the illusion, the feathery Eden.

So when your mother died of black diphtheria
And neither quack nor priest would call

To give their pince-nezed ministrations,
You and your brothers wrung cold compresses

In vain for her wild brow, cleft her grave
Yourselves, thumped clods on her plank coffin.

Later one brother took to drink and drugs.
The other slotted the family investments

Into curt bankruptcy. Meanwhile your father
Tried coaxing ghosts. Table-tappings

Stuttered perniciously from the next room
To yours, harangued your shuttering deafness.

Sometimes you imagined you detected clues
To a code, but it was only the singing wires

Of the death of the aural, the eighth nerve
Shrinking from lack of blood. That fenced you

High on a dangerous peak of vertigo, giddy
But unfalling. You said you mourned a "lost

Imperial music". What you were emperor of
Was a domain you did not recognize

As worth the name: a kingdom of aspirers
Without wings, a thin parish of prophets

Without words – except for baffled Amen,
A scraggy choir without a common hymn,

But no man without music in the throng
And each man sawing at his own bleak tune.

In September

Again the golden month, still
Favourite, is renewed;
Once more I'd wind it in a ring
About your finger, pledge myself
Again, my love, my shelter,
My good roof over me,
My strong wall against winter.

Be bread upon my table still
And red wine in my glass; be fire
Upon my hearth. Continue,
My true storm door, continue
To be sweet lock to my key;
Be wife to me, remain
The soft silk on my bed.

Be morning to my pillow,
Multiply my joy. Be my rare coin
For counting, my luck, my
Granary, my promising fair
Sky, my star, the meaning
Of my journey. Be, this year too,
My twelve months long desire.

Lazarus

Finally (in this dream) the Roman
Thrust his sword right through me.
I woke upon a pain which would not go.

It would be futile to describe the days
That followed, to talk of flame and fever,
Of red-hot irons and the like:

I was on fire with pain. I bore it badly.
They gave me cordials of blue-flowering
Borage but the fever would not break.

The last time I came round the pain had gone:
Then, after the long night, at dawn
The window blurred back into darkness.

I know you would have me tell you
Of spirits standing in white groves to meet me,
Of staircases ascending to the skies,

But that I cannot do. I have grown old
With the bandage-marks still on me.
They show me what I was and what I will be.

As you go home you will think, "Death's secret
Was not his because he was not destined
Yet to be dead". I cannot say.

I only knew of nothing and that, too,
Was of the world. I limp in the sun
Knowing that other. Darkness has its right.

His cry that ripped me out of nothing
By my roots, calling my name, that brought me
Back to the spectre of the light,

That cry, I hear it still in sleep.
I come awake, but paralysed, my arms
Imprisoned in the sheet, my legs rigid,

Unshivering cold. Sleep-walkers move
Without waking. I wake and cannot move.
How long this lasts again I cannot tell you,

A moment or an hour. It passes when I hear
Voices, long silent, in the courtyard saying,
As once they did, "Lazarus, yes, Lazarus".

Fireweed

Even now, after thirty years, it
Prints small indelible blooms
In dirt margins between lots that
Long since lost their vacancy.

Once the walls were down, where war
Burned flat the town, next summer
It came from nowhere searching, a
Late mourner, for the discreet place

In which to stand. It broached
Unbidding corners, stencilled rubble
Mazes, cul-de-sacs of ruin,
Amendatory, solacing, alive.

Nowhere was there too thin or meagre
Ground for it. It multiplied
Until its spurted pointillist strokes
Softened the black stone acres;

Took to the air, fastened itself
In the infirmity of the husked
False hour of the town clock,
Offered its own slow interval.

Lingering in car-parks, sidings,
It seeds impounded in another time,
Upholds in hope's abeyance that which
Moved beauty from griefless lanes.

Winter Rite

Mother-of-pearl in cloud, the sun low
Over the holy island; the straggle
Of sacred timber flexed and crook-back
For the dark months' long assailment;
And the lake where the god sprawls
Sleeping under rotted water-lilies, weed
Clogged at his groin.
    Safe fish weave basketries
Of bubbles through his fingers.
Year in, year out, in this wan season
We bring him offerings: spears, axes,
Sickle-blades, bronze scoops and bridle bits.

We have given him prisoners
For his drowned army, their screams at the knife
Sleep-songs for his still warriorship.
He is a god, he knows our service.

We have taken the great boar live
Then cast it into his pool, fenced it
With sacrificial arrows. It threshed
Until it died for his fresh food.

Year after year before the god's lake freezes
We climb to his stone altars. They tilt
Above the lilies which were gold in summer.
We face, despite our fears,
The god's invisible three faces.
    We do not expect to see him.
He allows us to approach and accepts our gifts
With the silence of all gods.

Saying

Andiamo amigo. We think we see
What we would say. But we lie
Prisoners within those words
We happen to know, captives behind
Bars of arbitrary sound. We grind
Meaning to a halt at the cell wall.

Language, vocabulary, are not the jail
But sounds made ugug, ciphers
That lock one meaning in and exclude
All others. So we express
Exclusive interim reports, construct
A rough equation in makeshift
Habitual sound. We tap on the jail's
Waterpipes, signal through stone
And wait for the vague answer.

So if I say *Areft paradenthic slodan*
Aberra antelist mirt maroda
You say that I say nothing. Though perhaps
I name the god of all green vines;
Or name that process which makes wine
Cloud in the cellar when spring sap climbs
In its far vineyard, but name it
In an inconvenient language not invented,
Or invented once and lost
And now forgotten.

Under a Balcony

Giulietta, Giulietta, in Verona
At Via Capello Number 23, I noted
This under your balcony:

Six hundred and seventy years
Ago it was your eyes shone down
On this thoroughfare of the town,

Six hundred and seventy years
(he of Montecchi you of Capuleti)
And the moon fell under a stone

Between the river and the old
Fair-ground. New neighbours now
About the arch. On one side

Pierella, with women's skirts,
As centre-piece a white plastic coat
Shining, trimmed with false fur;

And Paradiso dei Bambini, azure
With Creazioni Lula, small children's
Clothes, doll-size leather caps.

Next door, Onestinghi, Stationers,
Pens with that guarantee we would
All seek, *corpo infrangibile*.

There never was such thing, broken
Giulietta. You lie not even bone
Between the fair ground and the river.

Where Home Was

Home was where the glacier long ago
Gouged out the valley; where here
And there the valley's sides cohered
At bridges that had no grace.
They looked the work of men whose blunt
Belief was that a builder's guess,
If good, was better than a long
And bungled calculation.

They clamped together the two halves
Of our village, latchets of smooth
Sandstone coupling the hills.
We lived by one of them, a dingy
Ochre hasp over the branch railway.
Nearby the sidings stretched in smells
Of new pit-props leaking gold glue,
Of smoke and wild chives.

On Sundays when no trains ran
Overnight rain would rust the rails
Except, of course, under the bridges.
We put brown pennies on the silver
Sheltered lines for flattening.
Under our bridge we searched a box
Marked *Private*. In it were oily
Rags, a lantern, an oil-can.

All down the valley the bridges vaulted
The track, mortised and clasped
Good grazing fields to one where the land
Widened and farms straddled the way.
These small frustrated tunnels
Minutely muffled long strands
Of percussive trucks that clanked
In iron staccato under them.

We'd sit on parapets, briefly bandaged
By smoke. The trains went by to town.
We waved our caps to people we'd never
Know. Now it is always Sunday. Weeds
Speed down the line. The bridges
Stand there yet, joists over a green
Nothing. Easier to let them stand
Than ever to pull them down.

Summer Mist

Branches have common tenancy
Arrangements, moving in and out
Of one another's air at the wind's
Say-so. Where their top joints belong
Is never clear-cut:

Except as when hiatus calm of August
Forestalls September. Then mist
The silencer happens into grey,
Mist variously impaled upon the land
Subtracts the pulse of colour.

On such a windless day two men, their
Voices ravelling its few hours, gave
And gave way in words. Easily
They could have sung together.
They knew each other's unsung tunes.

Dusk and the mist closed on them
In the last lane. Now one instructs
The other: "Remember that the wind
Will soon return, remember
You are welcome to my air".

Full-Length Portrait of a Short Man

A good fat sheep, unsheared, could have bolted
Between Will Bando's legs. They made such a hoop,
Clipping his hips to the ground,
I thought he'd been a jockey. He had the gait,
The boy's body. He strutted with careful
Nonchalance, past the five village shops
We somehow called The Square, on the outside
Edges of his hand-stitched boots, punishing
The bracket of his thigh with a stripped twig.
But he'd have slipped round on a horse
Like a loose saddle-band.

                    In fact, he'd been a tailor;
From boyhood sat so long cross-legged,
Picking, re-picking his needle as though piercing
Points of dust, his sewing hand conducting
The diminishing slow movement of silko into seam,
That his legs bent and stayed bent. His years were spent
Coaxing smooth drapes for praying shoulders
Humbled on soft-named farms, stitching Sunday-best
For the small Atlases who, six days every week,
Held up the owners' world in the colliery's
Wet headings. His box-pleats in black serge adorned
The preacher proffering the great reward.

Will Bando ate perpetual cold meat
At his life's table: doomed bachelor, burdened
With thirst as might have burned his natural
Good grace; though drink increased his courtesy.
He'd tip his hat twice to the same lady,
Apologise to walls he fell against,
Pat on the head short bushes that he brushed by.
The needle's eye of village approbation
Was wide to this certain thread. But drunk,
On a dark night, his welcome was a door locked
Early against him by his lank and grudging sister.
He'd doss down in the woodshed on clean sticks.

One Sunday, deep in the thrust of red weather
Wounding October, Will was in no rick or woodshed
We could find. He'd strayed before. But Monday came
And our feet snagged paths in the morning cambric
Of frost on field after field. Every hedge and dingle
Beaten, every crony questioned, gave echoes back
As answers. Days drifted him away. In vain we cried
Into the last derelict barn, hamlets, hills distant.
The evening paper in the market town
Printed our picture silently shouting;
And one of Will from an old snapshot with a stranger's
Smile badly re-touched to a false line.

                 Children at fox and hounds found him.
He lay in the broken air-shaft, twenty years disused,
Of the shut and festering pit, not half a mile
From home. Rubble and tumbled bricks
Gave him sanctuary. Fallen where an unended
Dream of shelter brought him, he had given death
'Good Evening'. His hat with orange feather
At the brim was in his hand. He wore his smart
Fawn herring-bone with the saddle-stitch lapels.

Tricephalos

The first face spoke: Under sheep-run
And mole-mound and stifling glade
I was awake though trapped in the mask

Of dirt. Counting the centuries,
I scrutinized the void, but its question
Stared me out. What was it I remembered

As, above me in the world, generation
Upon futile generation of tall trees,
Forest after forest, grew and fell?

It was that once the ease, the lease
Of a true spring saw my brow decked
With sprigs, my gaze complete and sensual.

My eyes (the second said) were fixed
In hunger for the whole regard
Of what might be, the god beyond the god.

Time and again the black loam blazed
And shuddered with false auguries.
Passionless, vigilant, I kept faith,

Invented systems, sounds, philosophies
In which some far, long-listened-for,
Long-perfect melody might thrive.

The imagined dropped away, the perfect
Knew no advent. My sight was lost in sleep
And that stone sleep was haunted.

Two living garlands (spoke the third)
Strove to be one inside our common skull.
They half-entwined the unavailing dreams

Fashioned from light that is and words
That seemed ours for the saying.
I await wisdom wise enough to know

It will not come. The inaccessible song
Upon whose resolution we, awake, expectant,
Yearning for order, lie, is the one tune

That we were born for. Its cadence
Shapes our vision and our blindness.
The unaccountable is my stone smile.

Lament for a Leg

Near the yew tree under which the body of Dafydd ap Gwilym is buried in Strata Florida, Cardiganshire, there stands a stone with the following inscription: 'The left leg and part of the thigh of Henry Hughes, Cooper, was cut off and interr'd here, June 18, 1756'. Later the rest of Henry Hughes set off across the Atlantic in search of better fortune.

A short service, to be sure,
With scarcely half a hymn they held,
Over my lost limb, suitable curtailment.
Out-of-tune notes a crow cawed
By the yew tree, and me,
My stump still tourniquèd,
Awkward on my new crutch,
Being snatched towards the snack
Of a funeral feast they made.
With seldom a dry eye, for laughter,
They jostled me over the ale
I'd cut the casks for, and the mead.
"Catch me falling under a coach",
Every voice jested, save mine,
Henry Hughes, cooper. A tasteless caper!
Soon with my only, my best, foot forward
I fled, quiet, to far America:

Where, with my two tried hands, I plied
My trade and, true, in time made good
Though grieving for Pontrhydfendigaid.
Sometimes, all at once, in my tall cups,
I'd cry in *hiraeth* for my remembered thigh
Left by the grand yew in Ystrad Fflur's
Bare ground, near the good bard.
Strangers, astonished at my high
Beer-flush, would stare, not guessing,
Above the bar-board, that I, of the starry eye,
Had one foot in the grave; thinking me,
No doubt, a drunken dolt in whom a whim
Warmed to madness, not knowing a tease
Of a Welsh worm was tickling my distant toes.

"So I bequeath my leg", I'd say and sigh,
Baffling them, "my unexiled part, to Dafydd
The pure poet who, whole, lies near and far
From me, still pining for Morfudd's heart",
Giving him, generous to a fault
With what was no more mine to give,
Out of that curt plot, my quarter grave,
Good help, I hope. What will the great God say
At Dafydd's wild-kicking-climbing extra leg,
Jammed hard in heaven's white doorway
(I'll limp unnimble round the narrow back)
Come the quick trumpet of the Judgement Day?

The Piano Tuner

Every six months his white stick brings him,
Punctilious to the minim stroke of nine
On the day we dread. Edgy at his knock,
We infuse a grudging warmth into voices
Asking his health, attempt to ease
His coat from him, which courtesy he refuses;

And usher him to the instrument. He entrusts
Us with nothing, disdains, from his black tent,
Our extended hands where the awkward staircase
Bends, rattles the banisters with his bag,
Crabs past the chairs. Finally at the keyboard
He discharges quick arpeggios of judgement.

"As I expected," he says, dismissing us;
And before we close the door excludes us
Further, intent in his flummox of strange tools
And a language beyond us. He begins to adjust
And insist on the quotients and ratios
Of order in encased reverberant wire.

All morning, then, downstairs we cower;
The thin thunder of decibels, octaves slowly
Made absolute, which will not break into storm,
Dividing us from him. The house is not the same
Until long after he leaves, having made one thing
Perfect. "Now play," say his starched eyes.

Nearly Jilted

Tales of your unhappy wedding day
Were common gossip in that place
Where every slip was saga.
There was no child, there never would be.
It was simply that first promises
Were reconsidered. That old battle-axe,
Your mother, bore in, as she always
Would and did, as your young face fell.
And he, no man, married you
Without love and without pride.

Small wonder then that, after the rough
Surgery to your first sickness, the wound
Would not heal, though you clutched
The vile and burning bluestone to your body;
That, as you half-smiled, meaningless
Pain ground on over forty years
To bring you finally to death-bed.
Not the same wound, a different disease
Entirely, he said, burying you, his wife.
It was not his wound, it was not his life.

Section from an Elegy (for Dylan Thomas)

Dear drinking friend of the public bar,
For twenty years you have been alone
Without a drop in the black parlour.

You slipped away as though to place
A nimble shilling on a certainty
(One of your golden horses with three legs),

Not bothering to return. We loitered
In snug company. Jibbing the slow crawl home,
You went ahead, forgot the bitter barrel.

But you – to whom an hour, a day, a month late
Were the same – would surely reappear
To take up the tall tale where it faltered.

Half your dead lifetime later I still mourned,
Still half-expected you. Any next day, please God,
You would stand in the corner, your glass raised,

Your head flung back, a cigarette stuck
To your lip like a white syllable, removed
Only to quaff or cough or for the defiant

Steeplejack raids into your tried thesaurus
Of laughter; with that badly-drawn Rubens hand
(Under the bookie's suit, your shirt-cuff

To your knuckle) yet conduct the concert's
Spendthrift conceits from most improbable
Beginnings to more improbable ends

Which could never come to grief. Yet through
Those broken teeth there could slip, too,
The muttered treacheries against yourself

And the grave misgivings and the murmured
Bad debts of breath. Dear ruinous deserter,
Death, old familiar, wintered in your blood.

Now you have stayed away too long below
At silent paternosters in deep dirt.
We shall not meet again to bend the elbow.

Boundaries

A black flag giving assent to spring's
Illumination of the book of hours,
The whiteness of my almond tree; in anthracite
Of feathers, this blackbird singing.

Each evening just before dusk, in festival,
His pertinent cadenza to the day
Defines his territory, marks his boundary
Under my work-room window. The pane,

A yard or two of air, that's all there is
Between us. All? Yellow flute, black performer,
He flaunts his beginner's luck, chiding, gliding
Through variations upon unfound themes;

His musical unconcern crucial
To the seeming accident of song,
His obbligato signature deriving
From ancestries of whistling, unanimous

With the blossom. He, hero of branches,
(Trick of his head) perpetually surprised
To be trapped inside what he whistles,
Inventing nothing, being invention,

Flawless as makes no matter, taunting me
To delight. He essays yes out of his history
Against all configurations of silence
Through the one throat he happens to have.

Evening adjusts the trance of sky. His spate
Of acrobatics on a three-line stave,
Sardonic, repetitious, can never be whole
Except as part of what I wish to be whole.

Music to him is custom. His easy tricks
Are my despair. I turn back to the page
Where my chantepleure is born already broken.
What can I bid against him but misère?

And yet the future is still to be done.
He stabs me broad awake with notes
Not of his whistling. Thus runs spring's rigmarole
With no song substitute for any other.

Certain Questions for Monsieur Renoir

Did you then celebrate
That grave discovered blue
With salt thrown on a fire
In honour of all blues?

I mean the dress of La Parisienne
(Humanly on the verge of the ceramic),
Blue of Delft, dream summary of blues,
Centre-piece of a fateful exhibition;

Whose dress-maker and, for that matter,
Stays-maker the critics scorned;
Who every day receives her visitors
In my country where the hard slate is blue.

She has been dead now nearly a century
Who wears that blue of smoke curling
Beyond a kiln, and blue of gentians,
Blue of lazurite, turquoise hauled

Over the blue waves, blue water, from Mount Sinai;
Clematis blue: she, Madame Henriot,
Whose papers fall to pieces in the files
In the vaults of the Registrar General.

Did you see in her garment the King of Illyria
Naming his person's flower in self-love?
And in the folds, part of polyphony
Of all colour, thunder blue,

Blue of blue slipper-clay, blue
Of the blue albatross? Blue sometimes
Without edge, blue liquified
By distance? Or did they start

Those ribbons at her wrists in blue
Of a sea-starwort? Or in verdigris, perhaps,
Blue on a Roman bead? Or in that regal blue
Of the Phoenicians, of boiled whelks;

That humbly-begun but conquering blue
Which, glowing, makes a god of man?
She who is always poised between appointments
For flirtation, what nuances of blue

Her bodice had, this blue you made
For your amusement, painter of fans and porcelain,
You set on gaiety; who saw, in the blue fog
Of the city, a candle burning blue

(Not heralding a death) but harbouring
A clear illusion, blue spot on the young salmon,
A greater blue in shadow; blue's calm
Insistence on a sense. Not for you

Indigo blue, or blue of mummy's cloth
Or the cold unction of mercury's blue ointment,
But the elect blue of love in constancy,
Blue, true blue, blue gage, blue plum,

Blue fibrils of a form, roundness
Absorbed by light, quintessence
Of blue beautiful. It was not blue
Tainted, taunted by dark. Confirm it.

The eyes are bells to blue
Inanimate pigment set alight
By gazing which was passionate.
So what is midnight to this midinette?

Ultramarine, deep-water blue?
Part of a pain and darkness never felt?
Assyrian crystal? Clouded blue malachite?

Blue of a blue dawn trusting light.

The Birth of Venus at Aberystwyth

Beyond the pier varicose waves crocheted
A complex permanent nothing on the stones.
The Corporation deck-chairs flapped
Haphazard unison. Most sea-front windows

Confessed to Vacancies; and on the promenade
A violinist in Scotch-plaid dinner-jacket
Contributed little to the Welsh way of life
As he played 'Thanks for the Memory'

To two small children and a dog. Without
Any expectation at all, the sea brandished
Its vanity. The one-eyed coastguard was dozing.
Nothing in the sky sought a response.

The occasional pebble moved, gave itself back
To the perpetual, casual disorder
Of all perfectly-shaped, meaningless forms,
Like pebbles. There was one beachcomber,

From Basingstoke, but he noticed nothing
Unusual either when far out, beyond
The beginning of the ninth (one could even
Go as far as to say the ninetieth) wave,

Dolphins who hadn't spoken to each other
For years formed squadrons for her.
Trenches of water broke open, deep
Where she was, coming up. Weeds fandangoed,

Currents changed their course. Inside
An instant's calm her hair began to float,
Marbling the hollows like old ledgers.
The sea still tells the story in its own

Proud language, but few understand it;
And, as you may imagine, the beauty of it is lost
In the best translations available...
Her different world was added to the world

As, nearing shore, sensing something dubious,
Something fishy in the offing, the dolphin-fleet
Turned back. The lady nearly drowned,
But hobbled in, grazing her great toe.

Do not ask questions about where she came from
Or what she was, or what colour was her hair;
Though there are reasons for supposing
That, when it dried, its light took over

Where the summer left off. The following Sunday
She wore a safe beige hat for morning service
At the Baptist Church. Even so, the minister
Ignored her as she left, and she didn't go again.

Letter to a Geologist

for Wynn Williams

When was it we last met? When the stag
Devoured the vivid serpent then wept
Jewels as tears, antidote to all poisons.

Or so it seems to me. You write
Of your November find, fossil coral
Within a spit of that house of yours

(Which is too far from me. The free hold
Of our friendship is at stake); the coral,
Bring me a piece of it, bring it soon.

I would place it with that other handful
Torn, only last year, from a living reef
Six thousand miles away in the Indian Ocean;

And, in the pairing, see what you deduce:
That once your Flintshire hill – for me as distant
As the Seychelles themselves – was tropical.

The shifting land you've shown me: off-shore
Islands in green counties; tide-ways
500 million years of age under the plough;

And desert sands stranded in river-cliffs
On Deeside, come from the Sahara.
If these could move, could not *you* move, too?

Come south. Ferns in grey shale speak of you
From my shelf, of coal measures we were both
Born on. Your nugget of fool's gold

Is paperweight over the dross of my draft poems.
I know that, as I greet you, mountains shrink
Or inch up; the sea-kings' beds are unmade;

But these are rustlings, mere cosmic sighs
Unheard beneath our breathing. Let us tell
Some part of earth's true time together soon

With a drink, a song – the lullabies you sang
My children, come sing them again before sleep;
Let us say to each other words of a common world.

I've grown too solemn, so recall your jest
Of Man's not really falling off the peg
Vertical, ready-made, in Genesis:

But should you, in the field, come upon Moses
Striding through cloud on a Snowdonian height
With new or adjusted Tablets of the Law

Please check the Lord's amendments
Before you raise your hammer to opine
What stone it is that they are carved upon.

Yours, as the mountains move,
                                    Love, ever,
                                              John.

Notes to a Suicide

I

Act Five, Scene Five: who is there left
To care? *Exeunt omnes*, barely alive. But no,
Not *omnes*, there's one still lying there
Just visible as the lights are faded.

Which one? The one who worked hard
Not to smile; who, when he did, had better
Teeth than any. That was him, the young one
With a heart like a snared drum.

Who else could it have been, given
The circumstance? He was the man
Who refused to initial the armistice,
Who turned guerrilla when the war was won.

That was the way he was. When he was briefly
The central figure he moved, stumbling, aside;
And when he had lines he stepped quickly
Downstage and mumbled. But our eyes

Followed him to the door. He had the last laugh,
It seemed to him at the time; his dreams
Were of silence. Why will no one come
To drag off his body now that he has the floor?

II

There is an endless succession of rooms
To which you are not admitted. Not that I look
For you every day, you would have none of that.
You are the total of all closed books.

I see you, from above (an aerial shot
You composed yourself), walking into the sea,
Waving. There comes a moment when
Only your hand can be seen above the waves,

Then you are gone, all of you. Once
You meant this as a joke, the only truth.
There is no way to return out of the sea.
This film cannot be run backwards.

Why, then, do I care? Most of the time
You had not much room for pleasantness.
Your industry was geared for the sharp manufacture
Of what most mistook for deliberate mistakes.

Design for a Quilt

First let there be a tree, roots taking ground
In bleached and soft blue fabric.
Into the well-aired sky branches extend
Only to bend away from the turned-back
Edge of linen where day's horizons end;

Branches symmetrical, not over-flaunting
Their leaves (let ordinary swansdown
Be their lining), which in the summertime
Will lie lightly upon her, the girl
This quilt's for, this object of designing;

But such too, when deep frosts veneer
Or winds prise at the slates above her,
Or snows lie in the yard in a black sulk,
That the embroidered cover, couched
And applied with pennants of green silk,

Will still be warm enough that should she stir
To draw a further foliage about her
The encouraged shoots will quicken
And, at her breathing, midnight's spring
Can know new season as they thicken.

Feather-stitch on every bough
A bird, one neat French-knot its eye,
To sign a silent night-long lullaby
And not disturb or disbud her.
See that the entwining motives run

In and about themselves to bring
To bed the sheens and mossy lawns of Eden;
For I would have a perfect thing
To echo if not equal Paradise
As garden for her true temptation:

So that in future times, recalling
The pleasures of past falling, she'll bequeath it
To one of other of the line,
Bearing her name or mine,
With luck I'll help her make beneath it.

A Lost Word

In certain lights when the eyes, not seeking
Truth or effect, sometimes not even looking
Properly, see unfamiliar faces reveal
How they were long ago, young, fragile, special even,
Or predict, occupied with some thought,
Doubtless of no consequence, which ages them,
How they will look ten or twenty years hence;

And when sounds which seem on the brink
Of augury hold back, a near gale from nowhere
Dismantling the house on a cloudless summer midnight;
Or when, alone, just as coals collapse in the grate,
One hears footsteps on bare boards in the carpeted room
Above and then a voice, unanswering now, from where
It called and a shadow moved on the stairs;

One cannot escape the feeling that something
Almost at hand eludes us, that characters imprinted
On the other side of a page, in parallel, press through
On what we are trying to say, and would disclose
News or perhaps solace, some almost obvious
Simple sentence which would complete
The heart's short story of magnificence.

It would be good to believe that those strange faces
Were known once, loved maybe; that if we could find
The upstairs walkers hiding in a wardrobe
Or some cupboard and tease them from their silly shame
At being found, that stammering with surprise
At being discovered at all, or from long silence,
Unsure of their lines, they would give us the lost word.

Unable to sleep, shaving at half-dawn,
Unwilling to gaze full into the eyes
Of the latest forgery in the bathroom mirror,
Today's bad copy of an earlier work,
I have no lust for secrets. It is enough that the blade
Is sharp, that the sun lurks then rises over my garden's
Blown roses and its brown turmoil of leaves.

Captive Unicorn

His bones are red from lady's bedstraw.
He is fed, too, according to season,
Dry meadow-rue, juiceless rest-harrow.

Enchanter's nightshade made him docile.
He was led abject, pathetic
In jewelled collar, into this palisade.

The stains on his flanks are not of blood;
The bursting pomegranates spill their seeds
From the tree where he's tethered.

He day-dreams of jack-by-the-hedge, lances
Of goldenrod to crunch on, tangled
Heart's ease, salads of nipple-wort.

His nightmares are acres of fool's parsley.
He wakes hungry for self-heal
And the clingings of traveller's joy.

Released in winter, he does not stray.
The tip of his horn a blind periscope,
He trembles in sweet dung under deep snow.

Night in a Hundred

Cantre'r Gwaelod

Everywhere revellers, wassailers,
In a real spectacular; and surly
Beyond the wall, the devious sea,
That other great leveller.

Out in the midnight air, sleepless
With gripe, the town's teetotaller
Heard what he took to be voices
Crying, over the water, of vengeance.

He tried talking the rest into sense.
They ordered more wine to be brought.
Ashen of pallor, the servant returned
With a tale of fish in the cellar.

But glasses were recharged. The harper
Was made to play, over again,
The same old tunes of victories
Which had always been meaningless.

The company, maudlin and drooling,
Tottering from pillar to pillar,
Slewed off to bed, slurring and reeling.
Then the chairs floated up to the ceiling.

All round the town the scenes had been
Similar; guzzlers in every parlour,
The sea lapping at their squalor.
In came the hungriest roller.

At dawn there was only the blank acreage
Of the sea, with the harp drifting on it;
The stuff of a new sad song
Which proved to be popular.

An Ending

Lady, so long since gone, I am in limbo
Between an instinct of the dark, the sense
My own unfinished time has brought me to
And what you said you saw, and seemed to see,
On your last day. Feeling the faint pang
Of expensive appetite which, it appears,
Grates in the dying, you sent me running
For chicken and champagne. A whim, a delusion
Of hunger, that's all it was. When I returned
You saw things which I could not see.

"Aren't the flowers dark?" you said
Of the four yellow chrysanthemums which exploded
Pom-poms of formal light in silence
Under the black beams of that living-room
Turned sick-room; the ceiling the floor, too,
Of the empty room above in which you were born.

No one, I think now, could have invented
Such death-bed syllables. For then you said
(The poisoned, visionary words
Falling into the place of shining,
The chest of drawers, the cold brasses alive
At twitching firelight, the ticking clock
By the chimney stilled for your sleeping,
This place of much of your living
Which you had cleaned – how often? –
With cloth and polish and broom),
"I can see dust on everything".

But far away you were gliding into a long beyond
Of snows, of future weather's total indifference,
Of your own uncaring. I held you in my arms
As you were dying, with no sense then of a need,
As now, which would ask, *Why, where, these words
From one so prosaic, so afraid of any ending?*

Then you'd return with small apologies;
The sliced white chicken-breast unwanted,
The wine, in a kitchen cup to disguise
This once in a poor lifetime's last libation,
Spurned, too. Again, in shadows of shadows,
Which I believed you saw, you perceived not ease
But some uncounted-on and unaccountable
Glimpse of a pleasantness which made you say,
You who had been so afraid of your own eyes' closing
(Too easily persuaded, so I thought, of the goodness
Of this death – yet, was there someone there
Whose known gaze met your own?), "Well, well, well,
What a surprise, what a surprise".

At last, in my arms still, those far snows
Finally kept you. The rituals done,
We stayed that night in the house alone together.
Neighbours fussed, grudgingly left us
Each with the other. I had no fear, mother.

And it was in my waking that I heard them,
My neighbours making up their morning fires
On either side. In the same world as them
I went down into the day that they and I would wear,
The winter sun's new garment. Into the room where you lay
I entered, took back the sheet from your face
And, without grief, grateful for your easy going,
Gave you the token of love you were aware
No longer of, the kiss you could not share.
Forgive me for what happened then.
My lips upon your forehead tasted the foul grave
And I spat it to my hand and rushed
To wash the error from my proud flesh.

Note Found on a Mantelpiece

Welcome: the house greets you, is yours
For as long as you're able to stay,
Somewhere or other here
There are most things you'll require
From improvised day to day.
We have our special places
For this and that, of course,
But don't be bound by them. And, yes,
There *are* secrets lying about
In the backs of the darker drawers.
If you happen to come on one
Don't feel a guilty guest;
Let it be yours, too,
If you should wish it so, and can
Decipher it. It won't be missed.
There are others so well hidden
We're surprised ourselves when they fall
From behind a shelf or wherever…
Please help yourself in the garden.
Nothing's forbidden.
Upstairs, the big bed's best.
There are no noises in the night
As far as we're aware (unless
You've brought your own,
Some nightmare or poltergeist),
Except for the chimes in the hall,
Foreshadowing doom with their din.
No doubt you'll get not to hear them
Just when you've settled in,
As your time runs out and you're going.

Homing Pigeons

Out of a parsimony of space unclenched,
Into the not known and yet familiar,
They ascend out of their hunger, venture
A few tentative arcs, donate new
Circumflexions to the order of strange sky;
Then blend to a common tangent and so render
Themselves to the essence of what they are.

What beguilement shepherds the heart home?
Not what we know but some late lode-stone
Which, far, was always there, drawing us
To a meaning irreducible, to a fixed star.

Why then the falling, all the fumbling
As tumbler pigeons, fools flying, with the most
Inept of masteries? But flying still
And, despite awkwardness, being, as best we can,
Committed, in the chance weather we approach,
To what and where, without a sense of reward,
We may reach and trust to be fed.

Patagonian Portrait

League upon league of thornscrub,
the receding pampa of dust
where the nameless Atlantic withdrew.
Another plateau of shore,
then the vaguest of break-ankle tracks
under an ochre cliff; poplars
screening a house.

        But not a house, a hut;
mud walls, zinc roof. Inside, so many flies
in a cloud in a darkened room, shuttered
against the heat, that the old man, blind,
remembering, accepts them as the world.

What had he done, I wondered, asking the way?
Strangled a baby, poisoned the only well?
Grudging informants hooked their thumbs
over their shoulders, shrugging direction,
never directly pointing.

        Him? Why do you visit him?
What can he tell you? For fifty years
(the last farmer had said, five miles from Gaiman,
his boots white with saltpetre
from his thin hectarios), for fifty years
that man has stood on the sidelines,
and never one of us.

        Now here he is,
talking inside his dark, reiterating jealousies,
enmities, scorn for the loutish Welsh;
mumbling, barely audibly under the roar
and flailing of wind on the shack, calamities
of the flesh: Oxford and broken health,
the wrong advice to the wrong person
to come to a sunny climate. So, for an hour
his mind rankles away in its great tiredness;

until at last
it delves up a lost pride.

He rises from the bench,
tentatively swims through the flies in his black room.
I follow him into the air,
and the furious eye of the sun.
A line of knotted string sags between staves
as handrail past the poplars. Here, at a shed,
a humbling fumbling of keys, a long unpadlocking
of a plank door. It gapes on a shoe-tongue hinge.
Books to the ceiling; tracts and treatises,
all under dust from the pampa;
Victorian bindings, geometry textbooks, tat.
He feels for a Bible, fingers spidering shelves;
and brings it down,
in two from a broken spine.

When I had sight (he smiles)
I illumined many pages.

In bad blotched water-colour
clusters of angels leadenly a-plummet,
maimed saints with faded yellow wings;
wormed and distorted cherubs,
Jesus in puce pencil,
apostles with faces in mawkish pink.
What did I think of them?
I say how truly beautiful they are.

There is one lovely object in the shed,
an orrery. Ah yes, ah yes, he answers,
silently groping to turn the tarnished handle.

The mechanisms jerk on their worn gears,
Small epileptic planets
judder and lurch around the central sun.
He extends his left hand over them as they move,
but is too wise to touch.

Landscape in Dyfed

for Graham Sutherland

Because the sea grasped cleanly here, and there
Coaxed too unsurely until clenched strata
Resisted, an indecision of lanes resolves
This land into gestures of beckoning
Towards what is here and beyond, and both at hand.

Walk where you will, below is an estuary.
In advance to a fleeting brightness you traverse
So many shoals of the dead who have drowned
In stone, so many hibernations
Of souls, you could be in phantom country.

But the tapers of gorse burn slowly, otherwise.
And here are rock cathedrals which can be
As small as your span. And, at the water's edge,
A struck havoc of trees clutches the interim season,
The given roots bare, seeming to feed on the wind;

And in their limbs what compass of sun
Is contained, what sealed apparitions of summer,
What transfixed ambulations. If you could cut
Right to the heart and uncouple the innermost rings
Beyond those nerves you would see the structure of air.

Tune for a Celestial Musician

Too long in deference to the dark
We have supposed alert and dulcet
Devices, acquired by private miracle,
Were his, making his music oracle;

That passing the open door of his studio
In the sky we should see him swinging in space,
That disguising our tears we should cry,
"Play it again, Sam Angel, play it again".

Why? Were his five-finger exercises on breath
Better than ours? Are the more distant stars
His sounding-board? Must we assume a form
Always beyond us rankles to music in him?

No, he is ours; and ours his repertoire
Of stances. We dreamed his execution
Out of our fear of silence. Morning after morning
Sees him die as midnight after midnight

Re-invents him. Bring down his instrument
From the clouds; lute, lyre, whatever it is
He holds, with each impossible string.
His tune is of our own imagining.

The Gift

From where, from whom? Why ask, in torment
All life long when, while we live, we live in it?
As pointless to ask for truth in epiphanies
That throb in the fire, rustle, then fall into ash;
Or why stars are not black in a white firmament.
Enough that it was given, green, as of right, when,
Equally possible, nothing might ever have been.

Where Else?

Where else is there to sing
Save where we are?
True that the imperfect bone,
Stricken with undefinable complaint,
Some slight flaw in the root
For which new spring and summer,
Proliferating, cannot compensate,
Is not the topmost nor the perfect place;
But here it is, accessible,
Not broken yet nor fallen.
It is the boundary at the utmost edge
Of what we have. Whatever note,
Shaken from our frames, goes out,
As when a thrush sings late
Into the renewal of dusk
Which is not his or ours,
The known's not only what the heart
Treasures, hungry for great privilege.

Keep close, keep close. In the night, dearest,
Frontiers are unobserved. Sentries
With no vast care, except for sleep,
Also unsafe, shoot into shadows. And the law is
(Drastic ill-luck) that their bullets
Wilfully go straight to the target
Of what's invisible by day. They stop
The phrase which was about to say, almost
Like a hair touching one's face,
Something of song, perhaps of the true
Nature of song; of how fragment and grace-note
Would be resolved with the next dawn-chorus,
Except that, silence now, the heart's hit.

As it Happens

The ones whose images came unbidden
Into me, brow, jaw-line and shoulder-stoop,
Whose faces I shave daily; the long-hidden
Similarities seen more surely later, the whole crop:

I have them and take them all, having no choice,
If not exactly gladly, vaguely seeing
The sediments of my bedrock there to be rejoiced in,
There being no alternative to being.

Year In, Year Out

By thorn hedges across sharp moonshadow
We climbed to the high farms,
Stumbling in frozen cart-ruts;
Boys beginning to be men,
Saving our words for clear carols.

In nearly-perfect beat, and barely
Breathless, we struck up annunciation
Of the New Year by black gate-posts
Under gabled ricks. Locked-in dogs
Racketed to dismantle the white barns.

Our last rubato notes unbolted
Rhomboids of lamplight into which we walked.
Small round silver warmed our pockets.
Dark beer burned our throats.

V

Among Friends

The cloud of clear wine, each questioning
Harmonious; even secrets of the spirit
Given up, ifs and buts gone quite soon
After the last of the third carafe.
Then what? The resurrection of seems,
Nightmare, daymare, whatever further hours
Haunt clockwork, eat at our fretwork meaning.
Then we come down to the intolerance
Of our dreams and what might pass for dreams
Given the safeguards of illusion,
Drops in the last goblet. Was there ever
Such red, such dusty taste of brief sun,
So near, so unfading? This done,
That done, drinking – how else? – alone,
I signal to you over an empty glass.
So the strict seasons pass,
So the strict seasons run.

Cat's Cradles

We shape string patterns, each design
    crossing from hand to hand
    between us as we play.
So, with light touch,
    your fingertips meet mine.
    You lift this loop then that
to intertwine and weave them
    backwards and forwards.
    You see that no stray tangles,
no accidents to design
    snag the game's progress.
    Intent, closer our heads incline;
your hair touches my face;
    between your lips I see
    the tip of your tongue's stillness.
Now, serious popinjay,
    when with light touch
    your fingertips meet mine
I grow impatient
    wishing to consign
    more than mere string to you.

Soon I relay
    adroit reciprocations
    of design less than adroitly;
and you insist this shrine
    of cord be finished first.
    What can I say
(again that touch, your fingertips at mine)
    except "Be quick, be careless.
    Forget these fine
adjustments to the thread.

Why not mislay one strand
    and let all ravel and slackly run?"
So that elsewhere, nearby,
    I shall not sigh impatience
    but breathe the air you exhale
when softly you design
    (your calm undone)
    how next you move,
when, with an even lighter touch,
    your fingertips and lips
    silence me, and consent, in meeting mine.

There There, Then

So, to a child sobbing
Following some petty fall.
There seems hardly a graze
But white with hurt a rasp burns,
Real though barely visible,
After such little distance down.

Does he then need to be told
That no huge damage is done?
No, rather murmured to
That (There there, then)
All's not irreparable,
That the world may restart

If breath's not held-back,
Hugged-back so precariously,
Refused as though for minutes
Before the next breath's taken;
That the shaken frame finds ways
Of healing injury that's none.

But why, child, why the fall?
Ah, it's useless to say
That that's a grave, bottomless notion
And all to do, in the end,
With gravity. The real pain,
Which cannot be exhaled,

Churns unexplained, is more
Than half-imagined. It lodges,
And was perhaps discovered
(And how old was the child?)
After such falling in the feigned
Mildness of a garden where the stones,

Sharp for the first time, chose
Edges at that instant of descent.
It's no help now to suppose
That, when the first tree grew
Up from the seed of nothing,
No hurt, no mortal harm was meant.

Certain Episodes Reported with No Offence Meant to God

I. Sunday Morning Lie-in

On the seventh day he lay down
In a corner of what he had made,
Whatever it was. The place where he dropped,
Numb from his labour, was a desert,
The rubble and this and that of the builder's yard.
And now he was oblivion. He was night.

"Which way?" There came a voice,
That of a holy man, a long time later,
Seeking the god's face, asking
The emptiness of the wilderness,

"Which way?" Endlessly piteous, the mewling
Shifted sand that had silted the god's ears.
His elbows to his head, the god turned over
As mountain chains rose up and the earth shook.

Again, again, "Which way? Which the true way?"
The voice in its own torment
Until the god relented. For the first time
And the last the god spoke.

Go away, I do not hear you. Let me sleep.
Know I am deaf. Know that when I began
To make what stands about you
I gave away my hearing, dispersed it among men.
You ask me the true way.
Go and ask men.

2. Poste Restante, Counter Closed

The terrible noise of the first thunder,
The noise of something enormous
Crashing from quite a height.
So the god looked down from a particularly
Distant place he had constructed. He decided
That even the noise of unimportant fallings
Could divert him in his loneliness.
The noise was the noise of Adam leaving Eden
Without a forwarding address.

3. Entropy Revisited

The second law of thermodynamics
Discovered by some clever dicks
Who should have known better than
To report their findings in *Nature*
Was not exactly as god intended
It to turn out. All that bit
About matter moving from order
Towards further disorder gave god a shock
To read it in cold print.
Not what I meant, he said
Not at all what I meant.

Nobody heard him. Atoms tore apart,
Breaking their hearts. Chaos
Began to reign in the firmament.

A man with a violin
And a heavy moustache listened
As a train on a nearby railway
Hooted in passing and, passing,
Changed its note.
The notion of time came forth
And was duly mute.

4. Quo Vadis?

God got lost on his way home,
No one to tell him the way, of course.
No use asking man.
He suffered a tiny pang of remorse;
Another million galaxies were born.

5. Song of Anti-Matter

Oh dear, what can this matter be?
It's all right here in a negative galaxy,
But elsewhere, on the wrong side of symmetry, shatters me.
    Positrons always play fair.

Do not confuse me with black holes at large
In the graveyard of stars, the whirlpools that gorge
Events to non-happening. My opposite charge
    Is gratis, electric and free.

And when I collide with my sister, real matter,
We both disappear with a hell of a clatter,
Which tends to prove god is as mad as a hatter,
    And our E is the square of mc.

But neutrons, electrons and protons at play,
When it comes to the end, the last cinders of clay,
And the cosmos collapses, I might get my way
    And flare a new infinity.

Oh dear, what can this matter be?
Being a part of the universe flatters me.
But I'm real, a kind of invisible Battersea,
    See me or not I am there.

6. Ode to Winston Place

Hail to thee, Winston Place,
Former Lancashire cricketer,
Decorous at the crease;
Who, upon retirement,
Became an umpire;
But retired from this, too,
Finding it obnoxious
To give people out.

God, in your utmost hiding-place,
Let this man be a lesson to you.

Of Exits

for Mr. W.S.

In his *Elizabethan Plays and Players* G.B.Harrison says that Richard
Burbage first established his reputation as an actor in *Richard III*. It
seems that his performance was so sensational that even generations
later one Bosworth inn-keeper showed visitors around the battlefield
where Richard lost his crown saying, "And that's where Burbage
cried, 'A horse! A horse! My kingdom for a horse!'"

Yes, it's an old story. Actors – who better to know
Than you? – will do anything for effect. I swear
I knew one, he worked mainly for radio
(I'm sure I needn't explain), who would go
Out for a beer, a long way down to town, talk, joke,
And be back, not a syllable soon or late,
Without fail in the studio, exactly on his cue.
Master of exits, too, he got to his mark
On the night of his fate in a Force 9 gale
At precisely the imperfect second to be felled
By a falling tree as he paused on his journey home.
Give him, sire, when you see him, my warm regards
And a Guinness. He's a Welshman named Norman Wynne.
You'll find him, after Time, in every pub in heaven.

With Burbage, I shouldn't wonder, bird of a feather.
What they tell me about *him*, I see him clearly,
Going on and on about needing centre-stage;
Making up lines, as they all do, when they dry.
'A horse! A horse! My kingdom for a horse!'
How did you feel about that? Sky-high
I hope you hit him, simply sky-high.
They'll do anything for an exit line. I bet you'd pay
A lot to get that horse out the frame today.

Actors, give them their heads and they're off...
Only the other day there was a piece called
– Would you believe it? – *Equus*. You see how it goes on:
Over-inflated, arty nonsense, more wind than muscle,
High-flying pegasus stuff. And, by the way,
In this century there's more horse-power about
Than horses. I've seen Hamlets at full-throttle
(And full bottle) rollsed on the great white way
To being benighted, after they have done
Their best and worst, swaying house and body and home,
Barking, 'To bay or not to bay?'
In the sort of voice that didn't dog your day.

White Way? That's in America. You remember?
Though for you, I suppose, there wasn't quite
So much of it about. They have a thicket there
Of prickly people and trees called Hollywood,
And a ceremony honouring players.

With American actors the main factor's the will
To utter the deepest prayers for breath enough
To sprint up some shallow stairs, no matter
How old they are, to the summit of their careers
And the Oscars (they call them): small statuettes,
A barter of showbiz heirlooms, doorstops
For agents' bathrooms and actresses' bedrooms.
They ascend as their lives, like their teeth,
Are capped and falsely spanned with coy thanks
Which further cloy the awful tunes from a band.

On the way out, actors, when the last contract comes
For real exits (I mean) they're quite good at that.
Watch them console themselves and cherish
The chance of going off with a flourish
As the sole audience, that one black figure
In the back row of the gods, approves the final act
As they rehearse for the one big tacit role.

These sometime-sayers of your words; the true
And serious cabarets of sounds, which are the real poems,
What do they know of those? In part, in part,
You were an actor, yes, of course,
I see that. But, first and last, a poet.

(How could you stand that Burbage? *My kingdom
For a horse?*) I always say
Only when you can pen it
Can you act. And that's a fact.

Now this, *Ah, this!*
Let me read you my latest sonnet.

Castiglion Fiorentino

Given luck, not that such given luck
Is ever likely to bring one back
To see again what once one saw:

Here, although it is night, a near plain
With foothills breathing deep beyond, and
In the foreground eight nearly absolute

Arches, though the stone crumbles here
And there from warm geometries of sandstone,
Definitions of stillness beyond, the never-sleeping

Of cypresses and a prospect of calm
That the heart hungers for and the heart
Stops at, that is, if this is the place.

It is night, and there's no certainty.
With luck the landscape will lie climbing
Into beneficence of green, each gesture

Of land giving back the sun. There will be
No way back from its almost perfection, no way
To find its other version, except she were here.

Elsewhere

My wife tells me I snore. The night long
(To me it's hearsay, having been elsewhere)
She had played at in-and-out-the-windows
Of her poor sleep's tenement while I all industry
Felled an adjacent forest with my chainsaw.

I hear her dark-before-dawn report, and try
To stay awake in separate neighbourhood
To give her a head start towards the wood
That she would enter too – but quietly –
Patient upon the path her patience leads to.

Who is she when she is gone? In what season
Does she wander, under what leaves? What words
Does she utter before she returns, herself
Upon her waking, when what is not has contracted
To my discovered side in the warm bed?

Time to be up. The essence of who and what
Is mere quibble by easy labour of sunlight
Rebuttressing the bedroom walls so soon.
But a branch's wraith of shadow on the ceiling,
The question's ever-presence, clenches and trembles.

For Glenys

To tell you something I've discovered,
This letter from a land too far from you.
Believe, if you so wish, that the same
Distance exists between two persons
Or two points. It is not so.

I am further from you than you could guess
From the scale of a map or such weak
Atlases as we possess. By some inverted
Theorem of love I should be next to you.
But gentle loins and pitiless leagues apart

Prove me the converse. Old standards
And numbers are changed by the price of bucket-shop
Air-tickets, the stand-by flights of geography
And fancy. How, I wonder, having travelled
Without you, could loneliness cost less?

The far blessing is that not nonetheless
But more than less I love you; and discover
That perhaps we've been together for so long
That what my greatest need is is to be
If not quite with you, then in the next room

To you so that I hear you reply to some query
Even about a bill (though such questions,
You know, too well, are not exactly my style);
To prove that we are still the lovers that we were,
At war with death, its notions, and all bad weather.

Right Time

The tall clock still stands still
In the front hall, truly
My grandfather's clock. I inherited
His lost pulse and his receipt
For it. Now both seem small.

Its pendulum was stopped, its undernourished
Note given silence for every mortal
Illness in the house I was born in.
Its face saw out our lives;
Quarters, halves, the elaborate

Small joys and pains and sub-divisions,
Moment by gently-jolted moment,
Exemplaries of love, so softly then
As though they might disturb unwillingly
Another in luck in the next room.

A slowly-ageing present tense
Of nameless stars, which out of a brief
Clouding acquire a colder glance,
And yet with their thin snowlight
Alive not blankly timeless:

So with my clock's gilt hands. They tell me
A meaningless hour. The painted town
Above them with its green sea and calm sky
Has a sun at never-midnight. The stone
Weights were lost when I brought them

To this place. That old man, who sang to me
The hymns of all his certainties,
He'd hang his cap on the top crude
Wooden pinnacle on the high crown
Of this clock-case; every eighth day

Hoist the next eight with his black key
And be content. He and buried farms
Talk to me through the fled arithmetic
Behind these arbitrary numerals. This silence
Is true company, the painted sands speak.

Note from Cortona

Three o'clock. The small city soundless. Below,
A hundred tipsy roofs of medieval cards
Collapse towards the plain; but lightened now
Of their feather-weight of swifts skimming and nesting,
Might just survive another winter snowfall.
Two or three friends ask of you every day.

And each and cloudless morning I climb up
By the broken flagstone path where the vines,
Pleating the mountainside together, make slow
Melodies on its patient staves; the sweet peas
Gone, the blue moths' colour darkened
Into the elder. To-day at our stone table

I raised a glass to you. The sunflowers
Harvested, the haws scarlet as sunset,
I came down by the steep Etruscan way
Where the wind has flattened the wild white wheat
By the yellow cacti that are brown now;
When will their sisters flower in your garden?

I shall come home past St Mary's-by-the-Limepit
That the shoemakers erected, wondering
If that's one reason I return so often
To this high balcony of earth. In guilty absence
I greet you, and with a love
That's sharpened by my love of this dear place.

Storm

Thunder. Unlatch the front door and the back
For bolts to pass through without hindrance.

Lightning. Turn mirrors to the wall
Lest it stop to admire itself and then kill.

First, shunting of iron trucks in the sky, then
The flickering blast-furnaces tapped briefly open.

Four million iron bedsteads angrily thrown out;
Where will the Roman gods lie down to-night?

Chests of drawers shifted in all the mansions
Of heaven, every single floorboard ripped up,

A millennium of free coal going down tin cellars,
Calamities of guilt burying zinc sheds,

All eternity's ripe walnuts being cracked in two;
The impossible silver decisions, the last judgement.

Now the late bullets of executioner's rain,
The end of the world has come, and we but children.

We cannot hide in the cupboard under the stairs
With old coats over our heads, dusty and musty,

Counting the seconds. The sky is in charge,
The mirrors are blind, and the swifts stopped.

Evening in the Square

The swifts are invisibly mending the sky.
Where last night's wind tore it to pieces,
Stitching, delirious with light labour,
High on it, with dizzy double-darning
Done in twos. Such work's a tall order.

Clearly up there everything's still in tatters,
Total anarchy, a right old tangle,
All in each other's way. This lot need better
Management, a good union. But they are natural
Non-joiners, although they're fellow-travellers.

Darker. They're frantic with deadline screeches.
They'll never finish. The pigeons line
The high eaves, baffled. Get an agent for this show,
Do it with ribbons: a fortune. I'd do it myself
But mine is, alas, only a poet's licence.

Waiting in the Garden

If down into the green glaze
Of this evening garden suddenly cascaded
No less than angels, having been first
White hesitations, a small suggestion of cloud,
Then raggedly spiralling, trying to find formation,
Finally falling to be material, wingtip feathers
Transparent alabaster;

The beginners, good boys killed on their motorbikes,
In novices' nightshirts, shaming
The smiling patriarchs – who died before
The Bible was set down – as they clip
The tops of the lilac-trees, crash-landing a-clatter
In the rhubarb, snapping the stems off short,
Breaking their legs yet again.

What would I say if the aged, approaching,
Rubbing their shins, uttered "Come",
And then repeated it, "Come, come. We come to take you
To where the secret is"? Of course, I would ask
For their credentials; and they'd produce
From inside zipped-up pockets the required
Flying licences, innoculation forms and gilt IDs;

The old white-parsley-bearded flight-lieutenants
Delving for scuffed quill-written jobs
On parchment. They'd begin: *We the Archangel Gabriel,*
Foreign Secretary of Heaven, Request and Require…
And then their images, illuminated, faded Byzantine,
Their Wing-Commander, meanwhile, smiling a small smile,
Remembering how many abortive sorties he's flown.

And the young, the latest-risen from cooling blood,
Presenting their baffled grins from postage stamps
Of pictures taken in booths in the far corners
Of celestial Woolworths. You can see them jostling,
Fussing their hair, finessing with gold combs,
Crowding for next turn, excited. Smile, flash,
Smile, flash, 2, 3, 4. The curtain then drawn back,

And then the waiting.
What answer do they bring?
What answer not yet given by the evening light
And the questions and pleasantnesses
At the table in the green of this lady's garden?
And the strong white house, its books and pictures,
The questions and children I have pondered in it?

Would my most welcome visitors, awkwardly ascending
From their failed mission, be stripped
Of their silver stripes, be Heaven-bound not grounded,
Confined to base, forfeit their harps? I'd hope not.
Poor lucky souls, knowing the mystery.
I'd signal them "Good luck,
Good flying" as the garden darkened.

Illuminations of the Letter O

I

Brocade and embellishment
At the round boundary, a garland,
A gold-leaf beating of bounds
About the parish of snow:

Transfixed in wading the white acres,
Jailed in his pretty prison,
The subject of the text he cannot walk in
Is the sole occupant of zero;

Except for a statutory decorative bird
In permanent and stilled migration
Towards what words there are,
Yet mute when the darkness closes.

Between the snow and the page
Lies the matrix of the world,
But buried deep and inaccessible
As the mystery of the margin.

Shepherd seeking out sheep, probing
With his staff, examining the drift
Before him, or hunter trudging the line
Of hidden traps (for he is one or other),

A guest under grey heaven, one day he'll step
Into another meaning. Meanwhile he awaits
The coming of others to witness the poised
Mirage of angels over blank fields.

II

Of nothing and of wonder; of a line
Returning to the point where it began;
And all conjoined, three in a single token
Of zero and of joy and of no end:

Under unfathomable, regretless heaven
Dance in a round ring, syllables, your feet
Returning to the place of other dancers,
Nothing and dancing making the balance even.

Singing of burned-out suns, gaze yet again
Into the eyes of children passing,
Whose every glance reiterates the wise
Shape of all things and of nothing, the division,

The circumstance that brief breath brings us to.
Move seasons, die, unwind the endless coil
Of my unknowing; and when that same unknowing
Drops into nothing, give it its true name.

Turning

When would winter end?
The numb garden lay sentenced
In frost, all green long gone to ground,
As day by day, hour by grudging hour,
The birds grew fewer.
Day by day the trees thinned and darkened.
When would winter end?

Threats perched as strangers
In hawthorn and apple tree,
Magpies, unwelcome black and white
Patchwork, to be clapped away;
Even a sparrow-hawk perched, lurking,
As the solstice could not be
Coaxed on by the ritual of crumbs.
When would the winter end?

Then the clenched earth relented
And there where there had been nothing
Crouched three winter aconites, each
With five yellow fingertips drawn close
(A poised Italianate gesture), savouring
The sun; and then, surprised,
The crocuses' audacity, blue
Under the frost-burned rose-bush.
And winter's long watch was ended
Insomuch as each moment then
Hurried to the truth of March.

Soliloquy of a Secret Policeman

I am so gentle in my questioning
They hardly murmur as I hit them;
They proffer me blood in gratitude.

I show them true black in the muzzle
Of my gun. Nothing is darker than
The night trained under my sight.

We're a gentle family. My wife is proud of me,
(In the darkness of our bed her body is white);
"I believe in plenty of rope," she whispers softly.

I wake in the whiteness of our room,
Then flex before the mirror. Happy the man
Who goes to work with the bright prospect of pleasure.

It was not always easy. Once I sat
In the back of an armoured car shooting at children,
Jolted so much I could hardly hit them.

But I hit enough – and this was noticed
In the appropriate quarter (there is a justice);
I was promoted to Assistant Torturer.

The techniques are boring, and by now
Well-known. You will have seen
The basic handbook in the new edition.

My wife shows the neighbours the illustrations
Of me at work in the coloured pages;
The best are silver-framed on the piano.

Since we were told that the high readings
On the electric meters in the cellars
Mean nothing, I drive home with an easy mind.

Our rubber truncheons are dry-cleaned
Regularly. In the canteen I tremble under the glance
Of the admiring waitress with black lashes.

God has a strange sense of beneficence
(God, forgive me for that, but I have learned
That it is true). Was He trying – what futility –

To give them us as gift to compensate
Them for coming out wrong from His Holy Wash,
And this glorious country to be held in trust for us

Until we could arrive? Their future lies
In Education. Look, I can count up to six
On my revolver. She's a beauty, black, blank,

Black in the muzzle. Each time I take her out
For the evening, she smiles and blows kisses
In all directions, always asking for more.

Under whose hand will she lie after my death?
I have bequeathed her in my will. If my will's
Disputed, oh we shall be buried

In separate graves, my dear gun and I.
Dying, my regret will be
I did not do more to educate the children.

They hunger for the future. Oh, I dream
It will teach them the bloody alphabet
And to count One Two Three Four Five Six.

Tuscan Cypresses

Black-green, green-black, unbending intervals
On far farm boundaries; all years are one to them.
Their noon stillness is beyond decipherment.
They are at the beginning and end of the heart's quandaries.

On the darkest night roadside they judge the earth's turning,
On hills the brightness of stars is the brightness of day.
Each like a young bride is awake at too-soon dawn and
       hurrying midnight,
Yet each, like every death, is uncaring, each unknown.

They stand like heretics over long-decayed churches.
Some single as lepers are doomed to keep watch alone.
Fell those single ones, blast out their roots and detonate
Your only certainty; the curse upon you is whole.

They are the silences between the notes Scarlatti left unwritten,
The silence after the last of Cimarosa's fall.
They are all seasons, they are every second of time.
They do not improvise, all is in strict measure.

Though they reach to the impossible they never outgrow
Or deceive themselves, being nothing but what they are;
They know nothing of angels only of the enticement of hills.
They look down on lakes, the persuasive sea's vainglory.

They have seen the waters divide for divinities
But that was long ago so now peace possesses them;
Their only restlessness is the need for great annexations;
They would come into their inheritance by black growth and
       stealth.

They march over the border down into Umbria;
Their uniform gives no glint of the sunlight back.
As the gun-carriages threaten by they are the darkness
Of future suicides and firing-squads ahead.

Their solemnity is of Umbria, of burnt earth.
Even they do not know the bottom of it all, the last
Throw of the dice, the black rejoicing, the dying,
The vegetable lie, the audacity of bright flowers.

They barely respond to the stark invention of storms.
Enemies of the living light, they are Dido's lament.
They grow in the mind, haunting, the straight flames
Of fever, black fire possessing the blood.

They have stood at the edges of all events, rehearsed
Vergil's poems before he was born, awaited his death
In another country. Only the oldest of oaks can converse
          with them
In the tentative syllables of their patient language.

Lorenzo stood among them as the black-scarved women
Buried a child under cold, motionless candlelight,
The red banners of death and the white surplices.
Lorenzo would die soon, wasted, his wife gripping his ankle.

Are they the world's memorial, its endless throng
Of tombstones? Are they the existence of light before it
          was born?
That aloofness, that uncaring of what is and what is not:
Are they all spent grief at knowing no knowing?

They do not recognise this given world from another,
Having watched Adam and Eve limp from the Garden,
The serpent ingratiate itself into the world's only apple tree,
The silver rivers of Eden begin their grey tarnish.

They are the trustees and overseers of absentee landlords,
Keeping a black account of the generations of thin, uneasy
        labourers.
They withhold judgements and watch traditions die,
Are unrejoicing over the wedding party dances.

They have watched man and woman lie down in their vows,
        and wake
Into happiness made new by morning,
And observed the *contadini* setting out for the yellow fields,
Not caring whether they should return or not return.

They watched the Great Death blacken the land,
Agnolo di Tura del Grasso, sometimes called The Fat,
Bury his five children with his own two hands,
And many another likewise, the grave-diggers dying

Or running, knowing of more than death, into the hills.
There death stood waiting between the cypresses.
The terraces of vine and olive retched with the weight of their dying.
The terraces crumbled and the new famine began.

The cypresses stood over it all in the putrefaction
Of silence; silence of chantings dead in the priests' throats;
Silence of merchant and beggar, physician and banker,
Of silversmith and wet-nurse, mason and town-crier.

The cypresses stood over it all and watched and watched;
You could not call this enmity, it is the world's way.
Their stance seems set as though by ordinance and yet it is not.
It is merely the circumstance of the mystery, the reason for
         churches.

They are not everything, but they are trees.
They watch the pulse in heaven of cold stars
And the common smoke gone up from the body's burning,
They know the sourness of vinegar,

The sweetness and smiling of holy wine,
But they partake of neither in spirit;
Cannot be bribed into turning away, not even briefly.
There is no buying off their vigilance.

They are the melancholy beyond explaining,
Beyond belief. Accepting this, they are not tempted
To put on more than their little green.
Theirs is the dark of the unbelieving, the unknowing, the
         darkness of pits.

Some few are deformed, though fewer
Than in their multitudes and assembling legions
Their particles might have been heir to.
From birth their spines are erect, their outlines the essence of
         given symmetry.

Departure from this is brief aberration;
They must look down from their own escarpments of air, the wild
         lilies beneath them,
The wild mignonette, the dog-rose unheeded.
If they could smile a gale would storm south over Africa.

Each one is the containment of every one there was,
A compounding of all cypresses, of all their stillness.
They are the elegant dancers who never dance,
Preferring to watch the musicians, the bustling ones.

They are trees, but they are more than trees,
They go deeper than that. They are at the heart
Of the ultimate music; the poor loam and Roman melody of
        Keat's body
Sings silently beneath them.

What will there be of them when all men are gone?
No one to witness the seed of their secret cones,
The deep black seed, the seed beginning in Eden, coming from
        nothing,
From the beginning falling in Eden.

Only they can tell of that old story and they are silent
For all the long wisdoms have passed into them;
So, silence; since it all comes to nothing.
See how it all burns, all, in the black flames of their silence,
        their silence, untelling.

Saint Teresa's Drum

High on her bleak sierra of belief
To the beat of her dream Teresa danced
In the joy of her Christmas cold asylum,
    Ta-rum, tararum.

To the beat of her drum played once a year
(Barely a drum, more a tambourine),
For the Bridegroom's birthday this limping custom,
    Ta-rum, tararum.

Outside the walls of her barren garden
Rose the Paramera's saw-tooth scream;
She reined her tantrum blood to a due decorum,
    Ta-rum, tararum.

How far lost then her childhood velvets,
Cordoba's yellow slippers, the romances;
How long her chilblained journey's slow delirium,
    Ta-rum, tararum.

Bitter cold flagstones yielded up lost perfume,
Grace brimmed a fever from her feet
And her ankles golden-chained by bright laburnum,
    Ta-rum, tararum.

Then rheum, pyrexia of St Anthony's fire,
The fungal germ in the Holy Bread; the lunge
Of the angel's spear, love's tender pandemonium,
    Ta-rum, tararum.

In the wracked sanctum of her vision
The maimed dance, the submission done,
When would the Prince in His silken wisdom
Blaze dear in the doorway of her room?
    Ta-rum, tararum.

Blue Bath-gown

A night only but, in your absence,
Going to bed late from sleep
In my chair, I touch then grip
Your rough, blue bath-gown
And the softness of you is there.

How things summon up their opposites:
Heat cold, togetherness apart,
The staircase up the same staircase
Down; dawn dusk, sunlight and snow
In the one heart.

There's no dividing them. The bargain's
Struck with the first breath taken,
Sealed with the first kiss,
Broken only when the poor flesh reneges
And is its lonely self again.

Which dream, which dark? Which mirage
And which desert? I trust
The date-palm's sweetness, the tangled gold
Investment of your hair, the seemliness
Of your limbs, your warmth the cold.

Family Matters

for his grand-daughter born on his birthday

When my father would have been 98
Soon, soon I was 98 with him. When a century
Went by I was alongside.

When he was a million years of age
I would be abreast (glaciers move strangely),
Brother in nothing and everything.

"Don't be long," he'd say, going up to bed,
Slipping his shoes off, having banked the fire,
"Don't stay down too long."

But now this added bud, this rose sprung
Out of ice, this jewel, this abundance, this certain
Renewal of my birthday. This gift breathes

For the first time, cries her first cries,
Suckles her mother's nestling composure in
Her Katherine, Katie, *bella Katerina*;

New sweetling, silver's newest wafer,
Infant of my own infancy, sipper of beginnings,
Fallen into the ancient blessings

Of the old air's wine. I am this infant's
Infant, sudden beholder of origins,
The inventor, seeing them, of the first skies;

As soon, anew, my father lays his dust
Upon my shoulder, blesses with me the bond, the solace
For turning back to the flung seedcorn of the stars.

Notes to the Poems

Poem in February
Indications, **Grey Walls Press, 1943**
The first nine poems in this present collection retain the sequence in which they appeared in *Indications* under the name John Ormond Thomas, following those of John Bayliss and James Kirkup. Established by the writer and poet Charles Wrey Gardiner (1901-1981) and specialising in poetry, Grey Walls Press was one of the most active of small presses during the war years, perceived to be at the forefront of the Neo-Romantic movement and known in particular for the magazine *Poetry Quarterly* which Wrey Gardiner himself edited. He had already included the poem 'I, at the Channel' in *PQ*'s Autumn 1942 edition, when Ormond was still only 19 and just into his second year at Swansea University.
The Gloucestershire-born poet John Bayliss (1919-2008) served in the R.A.F. during the war. Associated with the New Apocalyptics because of his poem *Apocalypse and Resurrection* (which appeared in *Indications*), Bayliss was also labelled both surrealist and New Romantic. His collection *The White Knight and other poems* was published in 1944. Bayliss would become recognised as a significant literary editor of the war period, editing *The Fortune Anthology* (1942) with Nicholas Moore and Douglas Newton; *New Road* (1943 and 1944) with Alex Comfort, and *A Romantic Miscellany* (1946) with Derek Stanford. He later became a civil servant.
James Kirkup (1918-2009), a conscientious objector, went on to be a prolific poet, publishing dozens of collections; he was also a translator and travel writer. Teaching in Japan for 30 years, latterly as Professor of English Literature at Kyoto University, he became recognised as a writer of haiku and tanka. Kirkup came to public attention in 1976, when the newspaper *Gay News* published his poem 'The Love that dares to speak its Name', in which a Roman centurion describes his lust for the dead Jesus. The paper was successfully prosecuted for blasphemous libel the following year, when the campaigner Mary Whitehouse brought a case against its editor.
Poem in February had first appeared in the spring edition of *Poetry Quarterly*, Vol. 5. No.1, 1943, (ed. Wrey Gardiner, Grey Walls Press) under the name of Ormond Thomas. It was also the last of the three poems included in *Modern Welsh Poetry, an Anthology* (ed. Keidrych Rhys, Faber & Faber, 1944). In that edition, *Three Cliffs Bay* (their italics) appeared at the end of the poem. This bay on the south of the Gower Peninsula affords spectacular views in an area of outstanding beauty but, for Ormond, the association was also personal: his maternal family had their roots at nearby Parkmill. The castle is the ruined, mediaeval Pennard Castle.
Procession also appeared in *Wales* (ed. Keidrych Rhys) in the July edition of 1943. (Rhys had founded his magazine in 1937; it ran until 1949, and from 1958 to 1960.) This poem seems to relate to the deeply felt grief following the colliery disaster at Killan, in Ormond's own village of Dunvant: five miners were killed when, on 27 November 1924, an inrush of water tore out the roof and flooded

the mine. In due course, the colliery was forced to close, but the community bore the scars long after. Ormond would have grown up knowing about the tragedy because Killan figured in family legend: his uncle Emlyn went down into the mine to help in the rescue, while the heroism of Emlyn's brother-in-law, Willie Beynon, chief of the local mines' rescue service, was said to have saved the eight men who survived. The "blue mark" was the scar left when pieces of coal and coal-dust remained embedded in miners' wounded skin.

W.R. Price, a close friend and contemporary at Swansea Grammar School, has a vivid memory of Ormond – then in the sixth form – being much impressed by D.H. Lawrence's poem 'Giorno dei Morti' ('Day of the Dead', sometimes 'Service of All the Dead') and of him reading it aloud to Price. 'Giorno dei Morti' follows Italian villagers, priests and choristers walking to the cemetery for the traditional 2nd of November service of commemoration of their dead, when candles are lit in celebration. The ritual procession Ormond evokes is altogether more sombre, but may have been suggested by the Lawrence.

Bright Candle, My Soul
This poem also appeared in *PQ*'s Spring 1943 volume, following 'Poem in February'.

The Symbols
Ormond had a particular affection for his cousin Eileen Beynon, who had read to him a great deal when he was a small, sickly, child. They remained close. The dedication seems to be a gesture of gratitude for her gift to him on his 20th birthday some weeks earlier: the elegant Heinemann edition of D.H. Lawrence's *The Man Who Died*. His appreciation of its beautiful type-face and John Farleigh's striking wood engravings is an early pointer to a lifelong fascination with printing.

Poem At the Beginning in Winter, 1942
The dedication to Alex Comfort (1920-2000) suggests acknowledgement of a debt to Comfort, whether for his encouragement or simply his example is not clear. With Peter Wells, Comfort edited *Poetry Folios*, in which poems of Ormond's would shortly appear. At this time, Comfort was still only a medical student in the final stages of his training, but his poetry and his pacifism already marked him out as an inspirational figure. He was an active member of the Peace Pledge Union (probably how Ormond first came across his name) but, if they met, it would not have been until the late 40s. Comfort went on to be a noted physician and geriatrician who, in later life, would rue being known primarily for his book *The Joy of Sex*.

We Have No Name
Poetry Folios, not numbered but the sequence of dates implies 3, (ed. Comfort and Wells) Summer 1943 as Ormond Thomas

Before the Peace to Be
Poetry Folios, (ibid.)
These two poems were the first of the pamphlet-sized magazine's sequence of 13, which included work by Oscar Williams, Brenda Chamberlain, Keidrych Rhys and Anne Ridler. 'Before the Peace to Be' also appeared in *Poetry Quarterly* (Vol. 5, No. 3), Autumn 1943.

Second Epithalamion: Madonna and Child
Transformations Three (ed. Stefan Schimanski and Henry Treece, Lindsay Drummond, 1943) as John Ormond Thomas
Wrey Gardiner, who had published Schimanski's writings in *PQ*, must have been the link for him and Treece. Schimanski, who by 1946 was editing a small volume of poems by Boris Pasternak (also published by Lindsay Drummond), went on to work for *Picture Post* as Stephen Simmons (his name changed by deed-poll), but he was one of the journalists killed on July 27, 1950, when a transport plane exploded en route from Tokyo to Korea. Poet Henry Treece (1911-66) is better remembered for his historical novels for children, but it was his 1939 anthology, *The New Apocalypse* (edited with J.F. Hendry), which gave the movement its name. While Ormond was published alongside many writers perceived to be Apocalyptics, he does not seem to have categorised himself as such. Treece, who fell out with Dylan Thomas over the latter's refusal to be considered part of the Apocalypse movement, went on publish his critical study *Dylan Thomas - Dog among the Fairies*, (also under the Lindsay Drummond imprint) in 1949.
The Dunvant garden had masses of white lilac, hence the association for Ormond with purity and also snow. While this was clearly the only kind he knew, it is a confusion for those more familiar with the lilac-coloured *Syringa*.

Before the Saps Descended
Poetry Folios 4 (ed. Comfort and Wells) Autumn, 1943 as Ormond Thomas
Elegaic Nocturne
Poetry Folios 4, (*ibid.*)
The implicit relationship between life and death seems to have been an early concern of Ormond's and he would later acknowledge being conscious of writing poems which were "elegiac in tone" (*Artists in Wales 2*, ed. Meic Stephens, Gomer 1973). He supposed it to be a Celtic characteristic – the *marwnad* was a common form in ancient Welsh literature – as well as a matter of temperament. Over his lifetime, he would go on to write many elegies, or poems in tribute, holding that to be one of a poet's functions.

Strange within the Dividing...
New Road 1943 - New Directions in European Art and Letters (ed. Comfort and Bayliss, *GWP*) as Ormond Thomas.
When it appeared in Rhys's *Modern Welsh Poetry*, there was an extra opening stanza, perhaps deliberately omitted by Comfort and Bayliss. The *New Road* anthology included the work of Comfort, Bayliss himself and Kirkup, as well as many associated with the New Apocalypse; a separate section was dedicated to the work of surrealists. The poem 'Music of Colours: White Blossom' by Vernon Watkins – whom Ormond had yet to meet – also appeared, as did a plate of the work called *Rocks* by Ceri Richards. More intriguing is the essay by Kathleen Raine, a poet with whom Ormond shared poetry readings decades later. Entitled 'Are Poets Doing Their Duty?', Raine's essay quotes Virginia Woolf – from a lecture Raine had attended fifteen years previously – advising those who proposed to make literature their career "to defer publication until we were thirty". It's possible that is the original source of the injunction Ormond always attrib-

uted to Vernon Watkins and dating from later in the 40s, resulting in what would be referred to as his "long silence".

Funeral of a German Airman

Poetry Folios 5 (ed. Alex Comfort and Peter Wells. Barnet, Herts. undated but probably late 1943, or early 1944) as Ormond Thomas.

This poem was the second of a sequence of 13 poems by writers from various countries: Ormond's was marked Wales and followed Stephen Spender's 'The Conscript', marked England. Swansea had been subjected to its last major air attack on February 16th, 1943, when one of the German planes, a Dornier, was shot down by a squadron based at nearby Fairwood Common. On April 25th, the body of Obergefreiter Kurt Brand, the flight's observer, was washed ashore at Rhossili beach. His funeral was held a few days later at St. Hilary's church-yard in Killay. Dunvant – less than a mile away – fell within the parish, hence the event's further resonance for Ormond. In deference to local feeling, Brand's body was buried in a plot well away from Allied airmen, underlining how funda-mentally Ormond's pacifist perspective differed from most at the time. At the 20th anniversary of his death, Brand's remains were re-interred in the Military Cemetery at Cannock Chase, Staffordshire.

Birthday Poem

The Welsh Review (ed. Gwyn Jones), Vol. III, No. 4, 1944 as John Ormond Thomas

By now, Ormond had already met his future wife Glenys at University College, Swansea, and this was almost certainly written for her. He wooed her with poetry and, over the years, while his many love poems were dedicated to her, there are others which, but for her influence, would not have been written. He read his poems to her before anyone else and regarded her as an astute critic. Gwyn Jones, writer, scholar and translator, had founded *The Welsh Review* in 1939 and it continued under his editorship until 1948. In 1977, Jones included three Ormond poems in his *Oxford Book of Welsh Verse in English*.

Selections from An Elegy for Alun Lewis

Wales, No. 4 (ed. Keidrych Rhys) June, 1944

These verses were published just three months after Alun Lewis's death on 5 March 1944, appearing alongside two other poems in tribute by Brenda Chamberlain and Vernon Watkins. Ormond's title implies that the elegy was either longer or as yet incomplete, but no other verses remain. Although a paci-fist by instinct, Alun Lewis had joined the army and went with the South Wales Borderers to Burma. It was there he died from a gunshot wound, though the likelihood of this being suicide was not able to be acknowledged at the time. Ormond's film, *The Fragile Universe*, told Alun Lewis's story and was broadcast in 1969, marking the 25th anniversary of his death.

Let Us Break down the Barriers...

Modern Welsh Poetry, An Anthology (ed. Keidrych Rhys, Faber and Faber, 1944) In Rhys's anthology, this poem appeared ((along with 'Poem in February' and 'Strange within the Dividing...') under the name Ormond Thomas, following poems by Dylan Thomas and preceding those of R.S. Thomas.

First Sleep

The Welsh Review (ed. Gwyn Jones), Vol. V, No. 3, Autumn 1946 as John Ormond Thomas

This was the first of six poems (their sequence retained here) published under the heading 'From "The Influences"'. What others were intended for that collection is not known, he deliberately destroyed a great deal of work from this time. Returning to this poem more than twenty years later, he rewrote it rather than simply revising it and the poem is printed in its original form at this point, and in the later form on page 139.

Portraits of his Grandfather, of his Mother, of his Father
The Welsh Review (ibid.)
Originally entitled respectively 'Portrait of My Grandfather', 'Portrait of My Mother' and 'Portrait of My Father', Ormond made the changes for *Requiem and Celebration*, also putting capital letters at the beginning of every line, instead of every stanza. There was also some tightening of the poem for his grandfather. Under the title 'Portrait of a Shoemaker and My Father', the third portrait appeared in the *Little Reviews Anthology* 1947-8 (edited by Denys Val Baker. London: Eyre and Spottiswoode, 1948). Ormond was named John for the grandfather portrayed here, with Ormond a second Christian name. While there had been earldoms of Ormond in both Scotland and Ireland, in Dunvant the connection was altogether more prosaic: it was the name of the stationmaster's son, apparently taken from Derry Ormond Halt, a station on the West Wales railway-line which ran through the village. Whether any of them knew of Maria Edgeworth's 1817 novel *Ormond* - charting the eponymous hero's progress from poverty to wealth - is doubtful, though Ormond himself acquired a copy in later years. Adding an unusual middle name to an otherwise common or garden surname is a Welsh, notably South Walian, trait. Ormond was undecided about which to use in publications, hence some early poems appearing under the name Ormond Thomas, others as John Ormond Thomas. Early in 1955, his *News Chronicle* verses were the first to carry the name John Ormond and, later that year, when he joined the BBC (where there were already many Thomases on the staff), it was suggested that he adopt that form there too. He continued to use J.O. Thomas for administrative purposes.

The Unseen Blind
The Welsh Review (ibid.)
The hanging bell and the secret music underneath seem to relate to a theme on which Ormond would again reflect four decades later. In conversation with Richard Poole (*New Welsh Review* 5 Vol. II, No.1, Summer 1989), Ormond talked about hearing a church bell in Avila. He said: "It was the hour of vespers and the huge bell of this church I was looking up at began to hesitate in its ringing. The broad clapper starting to strike its sides less surely. The bell stopped ringing altogether, but it was still moving. Seeing this I found the moment very powerful, that living silence. Now, I say, the poem lies inside that silence when there's still movement going on, but the note is no longer sounding." In his *Letter from Tuscany*, written in 1986 and published in *Poetry Wales* 24/1, 1988, Ormond had also written of Cortona: "At one point up the hill at the time of the churches' vespers you can see no fewer than sixteen bells swinging and ringing almightily

from the five different towers your eyes can take in with a half turn of the head. A huge clangour and clamour. There comes a moment when the bell-ropes and wires are no longer pulled, but the bells go on swinging, the clappers still tinking on but getting slower and fainter; then come the short moments when the clappers stop reaching the bells though the bells themselves are still swinging slightly. It's the silence, the movement without sound that I sometimes feel holds the shape and music of unwritten poems. I suddenly think of George Barker telling me in The Black Horse in Rathbone Place (it was about 1946), 'All poems are at war with the silence that surrounds all poems.' He was right."

For the Children, Bronwen and Neil

The Welsh Review (ibid.)

The Angels in the Air

Poetry Quarterly, Vol. 10, No. 1, Spring 1948.

This poem, written in the winter of 1946/47 was first entitled 'Time, Even Violence, Decays', but bore the new title by the time of publication. Ormond included the poem in an undated, but clearly contemporary, letter to his parents, saying that it was concerned with the hope of peace and the future of the world, while acknowledging that this was a theme which was "not particularly popular these days". The letter went on: "It tells how peace can only be reached when every single person acknowledges his own personal responsibility for peace. That most people in their youth have been taught what is right and wrong and how they have fallen away from the truth. Perhaps you will show it to Granville [the cousin who had taken him to Peace Pledge Union meetings], I think he'll be glad to see it. For it contains a hope that these 'Men out of miracles' are still possible to meet. And that they can stand up to all sorts of violence and 'bursts of the blind skies' in the form of atom bomb or flame and still hold to the doctrine which we believe is the only one which can save the world. That is my job as poet (or at least part of my job): to show people that there is still hope, that with vision we may not yet lose all."

Expectation

Requiem and Celebration, 1969

The poem dates from the second half of the 40s. The relationship of poet and Muse was one which preoccupied Vernon Watkins and was, doubtless, a topic of discussion between him and Ormond then as later. Entitled 'Between Times of Silence' when first published, Ormond had changed this to 'Expectation' by the time of its appearance in *Selected Poems*.

Ikon

Requiem and Celebration, 1969

Ormond's particular placing of this poem within the first section of his 1969 collection tends to confirm that it was written during the time of Glenys's pregnancy in 1947, when prospective fatherhood found him looking anew at paintings of the Madonna and Child.

Windsor Forest Fall

The Welsh Review (ed. Gwyn Jones) Vol. VII, No. 2, 1948

For someone with such deep Welsh roots, this forest, with its Falstaffian association, might appear an unexpected setting for a poem. But Datchet, where

Ormond and his wife were living at this time, was very close to Windsor and they enjoyed walking there.

Doubts of Mary, Madonna
Requiem and Celebration, 1969
This poem first appeared under the title 'Sonnets of the Madonna' in the periodical *Life and Letters Today* (Vol. 57, No. 129, edited by Robert Herring, his editorial dated May, 1948). Where the original had a sequence of ten sonnets, 'Doubts of Mary, Madonna' has only nine: this and other changes apparently date from the latter part of the 60s. Italicisation of the first and last lines of each sonnet emphasised the fact that the last line of one becomes the first line of the next, while the very last line is a repetition of the opening line (a circularity also implied in 'Definition of a Waterfall'). The original poem, read by John Darran, was broadcast on the BBC Welsh Home Service, on Easter Day, 23 March, 1951. It was billed in the *Radio Times* as *Sonnets for Easter* by John Ormond Thomas, with the following introduction, probably furnished by Ormond himself: "Easter, the celebration of Christ's rising from the dead, is the theme of this sequence of sonnets. Poets have always been concerned with reconciling opposites and creating harmony out of conflict, and in this work Ormond Thomas writes of the dual nature of Christ: Christ the man who dies and Christ who defeated death. To heighten the sense of Christ's two natures, His mortality and immortality, the poet views the pattern of His life against the experience of Mary, His mother."

Sonnet for his Daughter
Requiem and Celebration, 1969
The original manuscript of this poem, dated 17-19 October 1947, has two titles bracketed together:
Sonnet for My Son, Garan
Sonnet for My Daughter, Eirianedd
Following the birth of Eirianedd – from early on known as Rian – on October 20th, the first title was crossed out, with other alterations made in blue pencil. Glenys had chosen the name Garan for its association with the part of Cardiganshire where she had been teaching and where the word denoted the heron (though, more accurately, it is the crane). While discussing children's names with Caitlin and Dylan Thomas, when Caitlin was pregnant with their third child early in the summer of 1949, Glenys said that they had intended to name a son Garan. Dylan, in particular, liked the name: the association, for him, was with the herons in the estuary at Laugharne and, in due course, they would name the son that was born on July 24th, 1949, Colm Garan Hart.

Midwinternight
New Poems from Wales, BBC Welsh Home Service broadcast on 9 June 1948
The poem was written in the winter of 1947/48, when he and Glenys were living in Datchet. The sleeping child was Eirianedd (Rian). The programme in which the poem was first aired also included the work of R.S. Thomas, Edrica Huws, Emyr Humphries, Henry Treece, Huw Menai and Vernon Watkins. In conversation with Richard Poole (*op.cit.*), Ormond said: "It's a love poem for the child. It also prefigures in some ways the paradox that's at the heart of many of the things

I do, or try to do, which is what Vernon Watkins called 'life's miraculous poise between light and dark', of the kind of mandala which I took a long time to get around to accepting as the only thing which is possible. I discovered, for example, fragments of Heraclitus, the pre-Socratic philosopher: 'the way up is the way down', the staircase is the essence of the idea that each thing contains the notion of its opposite. Hot always contains the idea of cold. Finally I found a resting-place when for many years I'd lost my former religious faith. I found that if you accept the notion of life you have to accept the notion of death. There are prefigurings of that belief, that attitude, that dilemma, in 'Midwinternight'."

Homage to a Folk-Singer
BBC Welsh Home Service broadcast on 1 February 1950

Born in Llangennydd [Llangennith] on 16 February 1862, Phil Tanner was always referred to as the Gower folk-singer. His was a weaving family, and their mill-home may have recalled for Ormond the roots of his mother's family who'd lived at Parkmill on the south side of the Gower peninsula. Ormond loved the narrative and historical elements of folk song and learned some of Tanner's songs himself. Tanner was the subject of an article he wrote for *Picture Post* which appeared on 19 March 1949, by which time the 87 year-old was living in an old-people's home, and this homage seems to have been written after that. Ormond himself read the poem on radio at the beginning of February 1950 and, when Tanner died less than three weeks later, on 19 February, he wrote the obituary in the *South Wales Evening Post*. He described Tanner's prodigious memory and continued: "He was one of the finest of Britain's ballad-singers. He would sit back in his chair, put his bearded chin at an angle and strike his first note, clean and clear as the Gower air. Suddenly the past was alive; legends, love-stories, pirates, sailors, Henry Martin, Barbara Allen (he insisted on it being Barbara Ellen), Fair Phoebe and the Dark-Eyed Sailor would be conjured up by a gesture of his hand tapped into life by his toe. At the song's end he would pause for a moment, then give the title of it." Ormond ended with a tribute of his own: "Contemporary poets are often accused of writing in an obscure idiom, of disregarding tradition; having acknowledged my debt to Phil Tanner in a poem I will say only this here: he and his songs made me more alive than any reading of poetry or study of poetry I have known. Time passes, and with it Phil Tanner: we are the poorer. Here was a man, and a sweet singer."

Dylan Thomas chose 'Homage to a Folk-Singer' to read in a personal anthology of poems by Welsh writers for a radio programme for St David's Day, March 1st, 1953. Though Thomas recorded the poem, it was not actually included in the broadcast, edited out together with others, probably because of its length. In his book *Wales in his Arms* (Cardiff: University of Wales Press, 1994), editor Ralph Maud's footnote to 'Homage to a Folk-Singer' clarifies that, although one list of the poems Thomas had recorded on that occasion only mentioned John Ormond Thomas by name, the title of the poem in question does appear in a manuscript now housed in the University of Texas, Austin.

For His Son, Unborn
Requiem and Celebration, 1969

This poem was for the son who would be named Huw Garan – known as Garan

– born in Swansea on the night of Easter Saturday April 8th, 1950. As the title makes clear, it was written in the days leading up to his birth.

My Dusty Kinsfolk
Requiem and Celebration, 1969
During the summer of 1950, Ormond's father, Arthur, was already very unwell, but what was referred to in a letter as a pernicious form of flu, turned out to be cancer and he died in early December. His father was buried in the graveyard of Ebenezer chapel and the poem seems to have been written following the funeral. Its last line gave Ormond the title for his 1969 collection.

At His Father's Grave
Requiem and Celebration, 1969
Ormond would have visited the grave at Ebenezer to place the traditional Palm Sunday flowers but this poem, with its poignant references to winter, was probably written late in 1951 around the first anniversary of his father's death.

City in Fire and Snow
Requiem and Celebration, 1969
In his article on Ormond in *Poetry Wales* 8/1, 1972, Randal Jenkins noted that this poem was begun in 1948 and completed in 1952. Snow fell in Swansea on the night of the 19th of February 1941, when the German Luftwaffe first dropped their bombs, hence the title.

Verses from the "Saturday Picture"
News Chronicle 1955-57
Ormond was still at the *South Wales Evening Post* when he began contributing verses to the News Chronicle at the request of his former *Picture Post* boss, Tom Hopkinson, appointed features editor at the paper in 1954. A photograph would arrive by post at home, Ormond set about writing and sent his copy back. The first verse to appear was on 29 January 1955, with the title "Saturday Picture: The Spiderman", in fact F. Bedrich Grunzweig's celebrated image 'Between Heaven and Earth' of a window-cleaner high on the United Nations building in New York. (It had already won Grunzweig the U.S. Camera magazine prize of 1951 and would be reproduced frequently thereafter.) Ormond's accompanying eight-lined verse, set out as two quatrains below the picture, contrasts the man working high above the city – the waterfront below him and the cloudy New York sky behind – with the "brunt and burdens" he must bear when earthbound again. While both figure and building are seen in sharp silhouette, with no "sketchy ladders" to be seen, it is tempting to wonder whether Ormond remembered this when he came to write 'Cathedral Builders' a decade later. 'The Spiderman' was the only verse printed without his credit; alongside that of the photographer, all future ones carried the name John Ormond, establishing this form of his name. Images of animals and of nature appeared quite often, but mainly they were of people and from all walks of life. What Ormond had experienced of the *Picture Post* ethos under Hopkinson – the commitment to an equal society and acceptance of a common humanity – can certainly be sensed in the *News Chronicle* verses. It is interesting to speculate whether, in creating the format, Hopkinson or his many German photographer colleagues were aware of the impending publication in Berlin of Bertolt Brecht's *Die Kriegsfibel* (War-

Primer) in 1955. This collection of what Brecht called his photo-epigrams, were four-line verses, each with a photograph, mostly taken from *Life* magazine. Brecht's intention was political: like a reading-primer, he intended the verses – simple but often carrying a blistering force - to help the viewer-reader perceive a deeper truth behind the war-time images, drawing attention to what he saw as their capitalist tone. Ormond's verses had no such agenda and were not social commentary, yet they do touch on some of his fundamental concerns. For him, they did not attain the elevated status of poetry, but the direct style, the word-play and sometimes quite philosophical note, surely make the verses small stepping-stones in the direction of his later writing. He contributed nearly a hundred verses over the period of two and half years; many he collected in a scrapbook, some asterisked by him when tentatively considering publication in later years. More may have existed (there are gaps in the *News Chronicle* archive at the British Library). Only a couple of verses had titles in addition to the generic "Saturday Picture", but Ormond himself gave titles to five published in an anthology for schoolchildren called *Dragon's Hoard*, (ed. Sam Adams and Gwilym Rees-Hughes. Llandysul: Gomer, 1976). That precedent has been fol-lowed for the selection chosen here.

Daffodil in Snow
19 February 1955; photograph by W. Suschitzky
Gulls
6 August 1955; photograph by G.H. Allison
Sow under an Oak
8 October 1955; photograph by Bill Brandt
Lovers in a landscape
12 May 1956; photograph by Maywald [Willy]
Mirror
1 September 1956; photograph by E. van der Elsken
A chimp gazes at his hand
15 December 1956; photograph by Joe Waldorf
Sonnet for Satchmo
22 December 1956; photograph by Gerald Pagano
Cuckoo in the nest
May 4 1957; photograph by Gerald Pagano
Father nursing Boy
19 January 1957 photograph by Henri Cartier-Bresson
Doe and suckling fawn
30 March 1957; photograph by W. Suschitzky
Cathedral Builders
Poetry Wales, 2/2, Summer 1966
The poem owed its prime inspiration to the Italian town of Arezzo, though not its cathedral but the church of Santa Maria della Pieve, noted for its massive, mullion-windowed bell-tower. When Ormond was in Arezzo on location in 1963, making his film *A Town in Tuscany*, he heard workmen singing high above him on their scaffolding and it was this memory that in due course triggered the poem. But it also had an association with the restoration of Llandaff Cathedral,

damaged when Cardiff was bombed during the second world war. Just before its re-inauguration in 1956, the then Dean of Llandaff, the Very Rev. Eryl S. Thomas, climbed the tall steeple to bless the new golden cockerel weathervane; Ormond, in an early assignment for BBC television news, climbed the same "sketchy" ladder to interview the dean at the top. The poem's gestation seems to have been almost subconscious so that, when it emerged in 1965, it came in a single brief sitting. In his *Letter from Tuscany*, (*op.cit.*) Ormond described the process: "it just seemed to come down my arm without my thought". Only a few poems would come into being quite so quickly; a similarly small number represent the opposite process, namely revision after revision over a long period; most fell between the two extremes. A typed copy has the title 'Mediaeval Triptych' above the title 'Cathedral Builders'. 'Design for a Tomb' was probably envisaged as another of the three and, though any such grouping seems to have been abandoned, by the time of *Requiem and Celebration*, these two are the first of a sequence of seven poems whose context is mediaeval. Over the years, it sometimes vexed Ormond that 'Cathedral Builders' should have become better-known than any other single poem of his (it still features most in anthologies, on radio and now online) but, by the time of planning his Gregynog collection, he had come to accept the fact with equanimity and made it the title poem of the volume.

Design for a Tomb
Poetry Wales 2/2, Summer 1966

Together with 'Cathedral Builders', this pair of poems marked Ormond's return to publication. The second line "Alas, lady, the phantasmagoria is over" was originally conceived as the opening line of an elegy for Marilyn Monroe, who had died in 1962. A note for a poetry reading calls it "an elegy for a libidinous lady to whose bedroom many had climbed one way". With "phantasmagoria", Ormond was invoking its original significance of magic lantern shows – invented in the 18th century, popular in the 19th, and a forerunner of cinema – as well as implying Monroe's rather extraordinary life, with its element of fantasy and, ultimately, tragedy. Glenys wrote that Juliet's tomb in Verona, which they saw when visiting Italy in 1963, was in part the inspiration, while Ormond's illustration for the poem (reproduced in *Cathedral Builders*) with its four-posted canopy suggests that he also had in mind another, rather more elaborate, memorial.

Instructions to Settlers
Poetry Wales 2/3, 1966

Ormond went to Argentina in 1962 with his BBC colleague Nan Davies to film the Welsh community in Patagonia, directing the three-part Welsh-language series she produced, *Y Gymru Bell*, as well as his own award-winning English-language film, *The Desert and the Dream*. The centenary of the Mimosa's voyage fell in 1965 and, that year, when Patagonians from Chubut and Trelew visited Cardiff, renewing friendships and reciprocating their hospitality served to sharpen the images Ormond had retained of their country.

Message in a Bottle
Poetry Wales 3/1, 1967

This poem was dedicated to the Pembrokeshire sailor Valentine (Val) Howells who, in 1960, had sailed his boat *Eira* across the Atlantic Ocean in the first *Observer* Single-Handed Trans-Atlantic Yacht Race. Ormond's 1965 film, *Alone in a Boat*, had profiled the man and his experience, with the poem growing out of their long conversations. They remained good friends. Val Howells remembers him one day bringing along a copy of Longfellow's narrative poem 'The Wreck of the Hesperus'. What does he know about the sea? asked Ormond. Not a lot, replied Howells. In Ormond's perception, as the final lines with their references to the desert and the hope of roses and wheat underline, Howells's feat chimed with that of the *Mimosa* on its even longer voyage to Patagonia a century earlier.

First Sleep
Requiem and Celebration, 1969 (revised version)
Following his mother's death at the end of 1965, Ormond was moved to return to the poem dealing with his birth so as to make a more explicit connection with her. That came in the form of a completely new final stanza of seven, shorter lines, which then necessitated revision of everything else. For balance, two lines were added to the opening stanza; the second stanza of the original was struck out altogether and almost all the lines of the remaining stanzas were tightened (mostly by excision, but with some word changes).

Poem in February
Requiem and Celebration, 1969 (revised version)
As with 'First Sleep', the original poem (page 47) dating from 1942/3 and perhaps earlier, seemed to Ormond to have elements recognisable and truthful enough to the poet he had become to merit reworking. A distinctly new element in the revision is the talismanic appearance of the ancient bard Taliesin.

Finding a Fossil
Requiem and Celebration, 1969
Ormond's curiosity about geology was piqued early on thanks to Wynn Williams, his great friend since university days. Well-versed in literature himself, Williams maintained a lively interest in his output over the decades and there would be further poems even more closely connected with him.

Three Rs
Requiem and Celebration, 1969
The style of this poem is reminiscent of Ormond's *News Chronicle* verses, though there is no record of it having being written for that series.

Tombstones
Requiem and Celebration, 1969
While there is an implicit association with the graveyard of Dunvant's Ebenezer chapel, the drawing Ormond did for Glenys's copy of *Selected Poems* (reproduced in *Cathedral Builders*) also suggests Ty'n y Coed chapel, Pen-y-cae, where her ancestors were buried.

Epitaph for Uncle Johnnie
Selected Poems, 1969
John Thomas was the brother of Ormond's mother, Elsie, named for his father, Ormond's grandfather of the apple-tree. There were very many good singing voices in the Thomas family; Johnnie's younger brother, Emlyn, was regarded as an even finer tenor.

After a Death
Requiem and Celebration, 1969
Like 'Tombstones' and 'Epitaph for Uncle Johnnie', this poem was written in the months following his mother's death in the house where they had both been born. Ormond's grief would, in part, be channelled into poems focusing on his early life, where the passage of time brought a different perception of the influences he had sought to identify in his early 20s. In conversation with Richard Poole (*op.cit.*) he said: "We didn't know what to do with the house; we kept it on for a bit though I couldn't afford it. You'd go in and you'd see the slug's trail on the kitchen floor – it's almost like a ghost-wraith when there's a silver trail in the scullery coming under the door – and emptiness. ... So it's a poem written out of deep personal emotion and it's got a note that echoes in other poems".

My Grandfather and his Apple Tree
Poetry Wales 4/3, Spring 1969
In annotations made for a reading, Ormond marked "Countryside, Mine, Chapel" as the three defining influences on the village of Dunvant, and wrote: "My family dominated by my grandfather. Such a strict chapel-man, vegetables cleaned on Saturday night." He also noted "Sung Short Stories": a phrase suggested by Douglas Dunn in his 1974 *Encounter* review of *Definition of a Waterfall* where he said: "Ormond's kind of poem is essentially that of the 'sung short story'". Yet Ormond was not able to look back on the old man with the deep affection children usually have for their grandparents. Determined not to replicate such a forbidding relationship with his own grandchildren, he decided they should call him "John" rather than "Dadcu", the Welsh name by which he had known his grandfather.

January Journey
Requiem and Celebration, 1969
This poem was written when Ormond was in Canada in 1967, working for the National Film Board of Canada, making a documentary on poverty and recceing locations in the province of New Brunswick. Rather than drive through unfamiliar territory in the depths of winter, he took public transport, partly for the opportunity it gave of observing people and eavesdropping. In the event, the film he made would focus on the Madawaska Valley in Ontario, where he was drawn to the contrast between the landscape's extraordinary beauty and the hardship of the people's existence. In the partly thematic order of *Requiem and Celebration*, Ormond placed 'January Journey', with its snowy vistas, last in the third section, to be followed by 'City in Fire and Snow', the single long poem of the final section.

The Ambush
Poetry Wales 4/3, Spring 1969
The characters and visual details in this poem correspond closely to the picture on which it was based: 'The Assassination of Saint Peter Martyr' in the galleries of London's Courtauld Institute. Dated 1509, this painting is attributed to the workshop of the Italian painter, Giovanni Bellini. It is sometimes referred to as 'The Murder of Saint Peter Martyr' to distinguish it from Bellini's 'The Assassination of Saint Peter Martyr', housed at the National Gallery, a more

familiar work sometimes mistakenly assumed to have been Ormond's inspiration. The poem also appeared in an anthology entitled *Responses*, published by the National Book League and the Poetry Society in 1971.

Michelangelo to Himself, 1550
Requiem and Celebration, 1969

In 1550, Michelangelo would have been 74 and four years into the rebuilding of St. Peter's Basilica in Rome for which he was commissioned as architect. While the title suggests the artist's injunction to himself – a reminder of the nature and inspiration of his own core creativity – it is also the poet's paean to the greatest of sculptors in stone.

After Petrarch
Requiem and Celebration, 1969

This is Ormond's rendering of Petrarch's sonnet 'I'vo piangendo i miei passati tempi', the penultimate poem of his collection of 366 *Canzoniere*, taken from the *Oxford Book of Italian Verse*, which had been a textbook of Rian's. The first four lines are a much freer translation than those which follow. The great lyric poet Francesco Petrarca (1304-74), was regarded as a founder of the Italian language as well as of the humanist tradition. That he was born in Arezzo, where the Casa di Petrarca houses the Accademia Petrarca di Lettere, Arti e Scienze, may have been a reason for Ormond seeking out his writing. Yet with this poem, and 'To a Nun', there is a suggestion that – having returned in earnest to poetry – he was deliberately setting himself poetical exercises in order to work at the craftsmanship that was always a prime concern.

To a Nun
Requiem and Celebration, 1969

This is a free adaptation of the poem 'I'r Lleian', the *cywydd* for a long time attributed to Dafydd ap Gwilym but now believed to be the work of an unknown bard of a later date. One of the great forms of traditional metrical Welsh poetry, the *cywydd* was much favoured by Beirdd yr Uchelwyr, the poets of the nobility, and is still practised by present-day bards. While the original poem is 34 lines long, Ormond begins his from the 11th line, occasionally re-ordering the sequence of ideas, thus contributing to its further abbreviation. Professor Dafydd Johnston, the authority on this period, has observed that Ormond's adaptation results in a significant change: in the lines "Your faith, my fairest lady, your religion/ Show but a single face of love's medallion", with Ormond treating love and religion as two aspects of an intrinsic same, where the original has one in direct opposition to the other: "Dy grefydd, deg oreuferch,/Y sydd wrthwyneb i serch". Joseph Clancy's *Medieval Welsh Lyrics* was published by Macmillan in 1965 and Ormond's copy is dated that year with his signature. Since Glenys had studied many of these in the original, it was an interest they shared.

The Hall of Cynddylan
Requiem and Celebration, 1969

This is a free translation of 'Neuadd Cynddylan', one of the sequence of poems from the ancient Heledd Saga. The narrator, Heledd, tells of the disasters faced by her brother Cynddylan, the 7th century ruler of Powys, and reflects on the death of her brothers in battle, near Pengwern, thought to be present-day Shrewsbury, originally part of Powys.

Landscape without Figures
Requiem and Celebration, 1969

As the first line indicates, Ormond made this a partner to his translation of 'Neuadd Cynddylan', prompted by exactly the sort of abandoned place he came upon when searching for locations. While the title of his television series on the early history of Wales would be *The Land Remembers*, Ormond the poet felt compelled to remember and, in remembering, to confer dignity on ghosts of people altogether humbler in origin that the historical figures being documented in film.

Froga
Requiem and Celebration, 1969

The poem's explanation of Froga's nickname – half-frog, half-ogre – indicates its pronunciation, but also points to its being the South-West Wales word *ffroga* (the Welsh *ff* pronounced as an English 'f'; the Welsh *f* said as 'v'). Ormond had evidently perused the ambulance books he'd seen at the Beynons' house: his Auntie Mary's husband, Willie Beynon (a man of natural scientific bent and an inventor), was a skilled paramedic often called out before recourse to any doctor.

Johnny Randall
Requiem and Celebration, 1969

This tale originated with Ormond's Uncle Emlyn, who, after working a late shift, would hear the moonstruck Randall, since Howells Row was just a stone's throw from the family home, where Emlyn too lived. Chapel-going and God-fearing though he was, he cursed Johnny's incantations.

Postcard from the Past
Requiem and Celebration, 1969

Definition of a Waterfall
Requiem and Celebration, 1969

This poem dates back to 1947: an entry in Glenys's diary for 26 January, when they were staying at her family's home in the lower reaches of the Brecon Beacons, notes: "John worked on a poem 'Waterfall'. Ormond then returned to it in the latter part of the 60s when compiling the *Requiem and Celebration* collection. It subsequently became the title-poem of the Oxford University Press publication of 1973. Ormond was careful to ensure eager printers did not add a full point at the end.

Elegy for a Butterfly
Poetry Wales 4/3, Spring 1969

In his commentary for *A Bronze Mask: a film in elegy for Dylan Thomas*, set against shots of butterflies pinned in their cases in the Natural History gallery of the National Museum of Wales, Ormond used the quotation from Chinese philosopher Chuang Tzu, writing in the 6th century BC: "I dreamed I was a butterfly and woke to find myself a man. But am I perhaps a butterfly who dreams he is a man?" While this poem is deliberately set in the context of everyday life on Ormond's home patch – Cathedral Road was round the corner – the episode recounted in the poem and his continuing reflections on the Chuang Tzu quotation set in train ideas which would emerge periodically in later poems.

Salmon
Poetry Wales, 5/3, Spring 1970

Ormond's 1965 film *Troubled Waters* with the countryman and broadcaster, Harry Soan, was shot in West Wales salmon-territory. It was here that Ormond first observed the particular rites attached to fishing, the starting point of this poem. But its gestation would prove protracted. It went through countless drafts and the dedication to the artist Ceri Richards (though it had not appeared in the *Poetry Wales* printing) points to part of the process coinciding with the making of the 1967 film portrait, *Piano with Many Strings*. (Richards died in 1971, and Ormond's tribute to him appeared in *Planet 10*, the following year.) In a copy of *Definition of a Waterfall*, annotated in Ormond's hand for a poetry reading, the words Roots : Death : Renewal appear above the title; a reference to the Fraser River (one of whose tributaries is called Salmon River) suggests that he may also have worked on the poem while on location in Canada earlier in 1967. There is also a reminder to explain that, in the final stanza, Gautama is Buddha, whose vision of Nirvanah came to him under the Bodhi tree at Uruvela. A more prosaic note says "fish allergy". Ormond liked to leaven his introductions wherever possible, hence the mention of his being allergic to fish by way of light irony before reading something serious. Cuttings he kept relating to icthologists' research into the life cycle of the salmon attest to Ormond's concern that poetic observation should accord with scientific thinking and not taking such a leap of the imagination as to distort facts.

Organist
Poetry Wales 6/1, Summer, 1970

In the opening of his seminal work *A Fragment on Government*, published in 1776, the philosopher and social reformer, Jeremy Bentham (1748-1832) wrote: "it is the greatest happiness of the greatest number that is the measure of right and wrong." It would become the basis of the philosophy of utilitarianism. Dunvant's fine choristers read from copies printed in tonic sol-fa (*solfège*) – even the cantatas and oratorios – hence John Owen being the only musician to read from old notation, the usual form of musical manuscript.

The Key
Poetry Review, Vol. 61, No. 4 1970/71 (ed. Derek Parker)

Publication in the magazine of the Poetry Society marked something of a milestone for Ormond. Probably begun around the same time as 'After a Death', this was one of a handful of poems to go through a process of working and reworking over some years. Further homage to Ormond's roots, to Dunvant's close-knit community and its intrinsic honesty, it can also be seen as key to part of the process of moving on from that part of his life, a poetic means of gaining closure. In conversation with Richard Poole (*op.cit.*), Ormond said that in this poem, he "set out to write with rhyme and sometimes deliberately deeply-buried internal rhythm. The lines had seven and eight syllables and so on. You write one strong stanza and then obey the form you've set yourself. But the overall effect was much too tight, rigid in the sense that there is no play in a meccano model. So then I had to ease the screws of its component parts as it were, and give it more fluidity so that it sounded more as if it were coming back towards ordinary speech rhythms and indeed ordinary vocabulary. But it is absolutely cross-rhymed with full rhyme and assonances right through."

Ancient Monuments

Planet 4, February/March 1971

The unforgettable sight of Llech y Dribedd, the monument which inspired this poem, came when Ormond was on location in the Preseli Mountains of North Pembrokeshire in the summer of 1968. For his film *The Bronze Mask*, he wanted to illustrate the influence on Dylan Thomas of the metaphysical poet Thomas Traherne and needed shots to go with the lines from Traherne's 'Meditations': "The corn was orient and immortal wheat which never should be reaped nor was ever sown…". After much searching, Ormond found more than he expected. In a 1974 article for the *Western Mail*, he described the discovery: "There it stood, the tombstone, the cromlech; a still island of stones in the middle of a field of barley which hissed and swayed and cavorted like a yellow sea lapping the grey, lichened monument. It was a magnificent sight. We did our filming and got what turned out to be very beautiful pictures. As we worked, I sensed that we stood inside the time of the windy, sunny morning, and that somehow, too, we stood outside time." Ormond sought to express that morning in a poem. In due course, he found himself running out of words for stone and asked the advice of his geologist friend, Wynn Williams. In that part of Pembrokeshire, Williams suggested, the stones could have been dolerite, porphyry or gabbro, for instance. Researching further, Ormond then came upon Alexander Thom's book *Megalithic Sites in Britain*. Professor Thom [1894-1985], not an archaeologist by training but an engineer, had surveyed cromlechs, megaliths and stone rings, explaining the mathematics upon which their layout was based. It was from Thom, to whom he would dedicate the poem, that Ormond took some of the evocative names by which the standing stones were known: Long Meg, Three Kings, Nine Maidens, Twelve Apostles. Increasingly intrigued by the theories, Ormond embarked on a film in which Thom discussed his work with the poet and academic Professor Gwyn Williams; from this beginning came the 13-part series *The Land Remembers*, with Williams, tracing the development of Welsh history from earliest times to the 13th century. The poet Raymond Garlick wrote to Ormond in August 1971, recounting his visit to Dolmen Bodowyr, near Llangaffo, on Anglesey and the "extraordinary experience of seeing the last five stanzas of your 'Ancient Monuments' materialise before my eyes. It's a superb poem. The chances [of] Bodowyr's being the point of departure of these stanzas are slight, but I thought you might be interested." Ormond's response to Garlick, quoted by Randal Jenkins in his *Poetry Wales* article of Summer 1972 (8/1), was couched in similar terms to the later *Western Mail* article. More than a decade later, a list of titles of poems in prospect suggests that Ormond, still fascinated by the significance of these monuments, was contemplating a poem about Gwal-y-Filiast, near Llanglydwen, in Carmarthenshire. Nothing of that poem survives, though he began a painting of the cromlech, its woodland setting highly distinctive and wholly different in atmosphere from those of Llech y Dribedd and Pentre Ifan, which Ormond had also featured in a different sequence of *The Bronze Mask*.

Paraphrase for Edwin Arlington Robinson
Poetry Wales 6/2, Autumn 1970
An early draft of this poem is entitled 'Gentle Rebuke to Edwin Arlington Robinson'. The American poet (1869-1935) won three Pulitzer prizes in the 1920s, but recognition came relatively late in his career. Robinson had suffered some hearing loss, reinforcing the sense of isolation which was a legacy from the unhappy, early part of his life. Ormond's sympathy may have arisen from his own slightly impaired hearing (which sometimes seemed to his family to be strategic: it was worse if he was distracted or grumpy), but he did suffer from Menière's disease, so that he too had known giddiness and vertigo.

In September
Poetry Wales 6/4, Spring 1971
This poem was written for Glenys in celebration of their wedding anniversary, which fell on the 21st of September. Penned late on the night of the 20th of September, probably 1970, because he'd forgotten to buy a card, it was deemed by them both to be infinitely preferable. Memories of key moments in their courtship are woven into the lines, while the storm door was the big black outer door of their home in Conway Road. The poem appeared in various anthologies: one which pleased Ormond was the *Almanacco internazionale dei Poeti* 1975 (La Pergola Edizioni) containing the Italian translation 'In Settembre' by the eminent translator, poet and critic Roberto Sanesi.

Lazarus
Poetry Wales 6/4, Spring 1971
This poem came to life, as it were, following conversations with Ormond's friend, Wynn Williams, who suffered periodically from the sleep disorder narcolepsy, together with cataplexy, the latter causing episodes of physical collapse. Williams's descriptions of terrifyingly vivid dreams and the paralysis which sometimes came at the beginning or end of sleep seem to have fixed that element. The poem was further prompted by a visit to Chichester Cathedral where one of two early 12th century carved stone panels – regarded as outstanding examples of pre-gothic sculpture – depicts Jesus's raising of Lazarus. An unsent postcard to Carol Buckroyd (the OUP editor who dealt with *Definition of a Waterfall*), dated 5th December 1973, shows the head of Lazarus, a detail from the cathedral's panel. Ormond wrote: "My Lazarus poem had been around in my head for a long time, and then one day I was reminded of it when I saw this version on one of my trips to Sussex. The poem got finished a few months later." The postcard's printed inscription suggests that the panel served to "convey a reverent feeling of wonder and compassion at the awesome moment of the miraculous resurrection", yet the poem is a distinct subversion of the New Testament. Ormond notes for a poetry-reading are quotes; the first is from Heraclitus: "The waking share a common world" (elsewhere expressed as: "The waking have one world in common; sleepers have each a private world of his own."); the second is again the butterfly/man quotation of Chuang Tzu (*q.v.*). Ormond also refers to "Browning's blue-flowering borage", the herb traditionally used to reduce a high fever. In Robert Browning's long poem 'An Epistle Containing the Strange Medical Experience of Karshish, the Arab Physician' –

an account of Karshish's encounter with Lazarus – lines towards the end of the poem read: "I noticed on the margin of a pool/Blue-flowering borage, the Aleppo sort,/Aboundeth, very nitrous. It is strange!"

Fireweed

Poetry Wales 6/4, Spring 1971

Fireweed is a name for Rosebay willowherb. It was originally less commonly found but, by the end of the war, was colonising bombed sites in London, hence its popular name among Londoners: "bombweed". During his time at *Picture Post* just after the war, Ormond would have been very familiar with such sites in the vicinity of Fleet Street, but the pinky-purple flowers also became a feature of Swansea's bombed areas, which long remained derelict. Ormond's approach to description was often painterly. The Pointillistes used short strokes of different coloured paint to build up a picture and, here, the word is used for the thin, spiky capsules out of which the ripe, feathery seeds eventually explode. The poem is an acrostic, spelling out the rosebay willowherb's scientific name, *Epilobium angustifolium* (though it would later be reclassified as *Chamerion angustifolium*). Ormond put it in his original selection for *Definition of a Waterfall*, where a faint pencil note in his own mock-up of the collection points out the acrostic, adding "not that it matters". His decision not to include the poem was probably because his lines, inaccurately, spell *epilobilium*, too clever for its own good.

Winter Rite

Poetry Wales 7/1, Summer 1971

For his series *The Land Remembers*, Ormond immersed himself in Celtic history and archaeology and this was subsequently reflected in poems. Headed "The Spirit of Place", jottings made for a reading show that the ritual, votive offerings enumerated in 'Winter Rite' were the Iron and Bronze Age objects discovered at Llyn Cerrig Bach on Anglesey in 1942, when a runway at the R.A.F. Valley's air-field was being extended. The "screams at the knife" relate to the custom of human sacrifice on blood-drenched altars to propitiate the gods, as noted by the historian Tacitus in his Annals (XIV, 29-30) when describing the Roman conquest of Anglesey by Paulinus Suetonius.

Saying

Second Æon Vol.11, 1971.

This journal of contemporary poetry, graphics, fiction and reviews, edited by Peter Finch, ran from late 1966 to early 1975. In it, the poem appeared under the title '*Andiamo Amigo*', the opening words. By its appearance in *Definition of a Waterfall*, Ormond had made minor changes, including cutting a couple of words from the phrase of indecipherable language, with line-breaks altered accordingly. The original also contained two final lines standing alone. They read: "All poems are at war/ With the silence that surrounds them." Ormond took these out, presumably remembering that they were words he had heard George Barker speak, in conversation, some twenty-six years earlier. He would remember them again, quoting the ending slightly differently, in his *Letter from Tuscany* (see earlier note to 'The Unseen Blind').

Under a Balcony

Poetry Wales 6/4, Spring 1971

This poem originated in the 1963 visit to Verona, where the balcony immortalised in Shakespeare's *Romeo and Juliet* is part of a medieval palace, known as the Casa di Giulietta, in the city's Via Capello. While the ill-fated lovers' story and that of their warring families had some basis in historical fact, Ormond's reference to 670 years was an approximation, chosen to suit the line. He also used poetic licence to alter the name of the stationers, actually Onestinghel, to Onestinghi, perhaps to give the internal rhyme with "guarantee" in the next line. The pens advertised as "*corpo infrangibile*" were allegedly unbreakable.

Where Home Was
Poetry Dimension Annual 1, (ed. Jeremy Robson), 1973
This poem was originally entitled 'Bridges', and the terrace of cottages where the Thomases lived (originally called Bridge Terrace, later Station Road before being included in Dunvant Road) stood close by the bridge over the railway-line. A typed draft with two rough sketches of bridges is dated June 18: 71. Ormond had by this time become friends with the poets Leslie Norris and Ted Walker, who lived near each other in West Sussex; their meetings sometimes prompted poetic jousting. This poem was the product of one such challenge.

Summer Mist
Transatlantic Review 42, Spring 1972
In his Conversations with John Ormond (*op.cit.*) Richard Poole quoted Ormond's account of this poem's origin: "I was staying in Sussex one summer and had a really long day's walking with Ted Walker up on the Downs. We came back to his village [Eastergate] and went to the local pub and had a jar or two, and as we were walking home – and we really had had a most marvellous day of conversation, getting to know one another for the first time – Ted said, 'All right, by one o'clock tomorrow each of us will produce a poem. You set the subject.' We were walking up the lane away from the pub on the edge of the village, and it's low country there and mist was swirling at about half past ten on the summer's night off the water. 'Summer mist,' I said, 'that's the subject.' And that's how the poem got written, overnight, and it's about friendship. I wouldn't have got it otherwise."

Full-Length Portrait of a Short Man
Poetry Wales 8/1, Summer 1972

Tricephalos
Poetry Wales (ibid.)
In 'Winter Rite', Ormond had written about "the god's invisible three faces" and the poem about the three-faced, rather than three-headed, Tricephalos seems to have followed naturally. The complex image of three composite faces was one he worked to capture in a pen-and-ink drawing, their features and their beards very like those of the poet Gwyn Williams with whom he worked on *The Land Remembers*. Yearning for life's defining message – "the inaccessible song" first alluded to in his early work – would become a recurrent Ormond theme.

Lament for a Leg
Poetry Wales 8/4, Spring 1973
This appeared in a special *PW* issue on Dafydd ap Gwilym, one of a series by different poets (including Glyn Jones, Gillian Clarke and Gwyn Williams)

making up 'A Garland for Dafydd ap Gwilym'. The lines prefacing the poem refer to the abbey church of Strata Florida, Ystrad Fflur in Cardiganshire, burial ground of the princely Dinefwr family of Deheubarth, and where Dafydd is said to be buried beneath the yew-tree. In a prompt for a reading, Ormond noted that his poem was a "cod" *cywydd* , and setting the beer-drinking Henry behind the bar is surely a nod to one of Dafydd ap Gwilym's most celebrated *cywyddau*, 'Trafferth mewn Tafarn' (Trouble at a Tavern).

The Piano Tuner
Definition of a Waterfall, 1973
A draft of the poem is dated September 4 1972; the only change would be to make the last line begin with 'perfect'. Piano-tuner William Hopkins lived opposite the Ormonds in Conway Road: blind since birth, he was fiercely proud and independent, his one concession being that his wife escort him across the road at the appointed hour. While music was a consoling passion, he had a forbidding aura. Ormond's note for a poetry reading reads: "We all have our black letter days, the day we're due at the dentist, the day of the medical check-up, the day the rates fall due…" To Richard Poole (*op.cit.*), Ormond recounted reading the poem over the phone to Ted Walker. After the silence when he'd finished, Walker said "I know which part of that poem you got first! And I said Oh yes? he said, 'The last two words: "Now play say his starched eyes."' Ormond recalled seeing "behind Hopkins's dark glasses the milky blue there can be in a blind man's eyes, and it reminded me of washday at home when I was a boy, when starch for the white shirts would be made, and as it got colder it blued over." John Wain's inclusion of the poem in his *Anthology of Contemporary Poetry*, (Hutchinson, 1979), marked its first correct appearance: the words "attempt to ease /His coat from him," had been omitted when it was published in 1973.

Nearly Jilted
Second Æon, Vol. 16/17, 1973

Section from an Elegy
Poetry Wales 9/2, Autumn 1973
This volume of *Poetry Wales* was a special Dylan Thomas issue marking the 20th anniversary of his death. Ormond's propensity for self-criticism is probably reflected more in his search for a fitting elegy for Thomas than in the pursuit of any other poem. He saw it as the only true testimony of friendship but, essentially, nothing was good enough for Dylan that couldn't be bettered. Despite returning periodically to the task over many years, he was never satisfied: drafts were mainly destroyed, and it remained uncompleted. He did not include this poem in *Selected Poems*, from which may be inferred that he was not happy enough with it, or simply that he was still working on the rest of the poem. Ormond's relationship with the poet seems to have been a combination of elements: initially a kind of hero-worship, then deep affection for a much-loved friend, to which was then added guilty anguish that he should have died young. The memory of seeing Thomas in his coffin, invoked whenever he saw the bronze death mask in the National Museum of Wales, certainly haunted him. While the definitive elegy would always elude him, he paid homage in other ways. Having taken part in the broadcast of *Under Milk Wood*, he contributed a

heartfelt radio tribute to Thomas in *Welsh Bookshelf*, transmitted on the BBC Welsh Home Service on 1 December 1954 and, over the years, on anniversaries and on the publication of letters and biographies, he made further tributes. Ormond made three films about him: *Return Journey* (1964) was the first; the second, *A Bronze Mask: a film in elegy for Dylan Thomas*, was shown in 1969; the final film, *I Sing to you Strangers*, broadcast on BBC 2 in November 1982, was his most conscious attempt to document the Dylan he had known. Ormond's billing for the *Radio Times* reads: "I Sing to you Strangers. So wrote Dylan Thomas in the Prologue to his *Collected Poems*. In this film, René Cutforth, some who were not strangers – friends, relatives and fellow-broadcasters, who in their various ways loved the poet – give an account of the person he really was. The portrait that emerges, enriched by Thomas's own voice in poetry and prose, is different from the generally accepted picture of the inspired and irresponsible drunkard who somehow received a commemorative stone in Westminster Abbey." As the poem suggests, Thomas and Ormond had indeed frequented bars together, probably in Oxford where they first met and then in Soho in the late 1940s, as well in Laugharne itself and Swansea. Yet one of Ormond's prime concerns, notably in *I Sing to you Strangers*, was always to remind people of the wit, the lively conversation and the great passion for poetry that was always at the heart of the conversation. He was also at pains to point out that, unlike their mutual friend Daniel Jones, Thomas did not take his drink well, suggesting that a new look at the circumstances of his death was overdue. Evidence vindicating that view would only emerge much later, long after Ormond's own death.

Boundaries
Poetry (Chicago) Vol. CXXV, No.1 (ed. Daryl Hine), October 1974
Early notes for the poem suggest it was begun in 1972. The dedication to Ormond's friend, author and playwright Peter Tinniswood (1936- 2003), was included in the *Penguin Modern Poets* collection but omitted by the time of *Selected Poems* of 1987. In his copy of the magazine, from which he read the poem while on his American tour and by way of prompt for his introduction, Ormond wrote: "What on this speck of earth, in an expanding universe, is the poet trying to do? I certainly look for, am satisfied by, signs of order." Another note reads: "*chantepleure*: the singing we do in this world which will bring us tears in the next". *Chantepleure*'s literal meaning – singing and weeping – is not unrelated to Ormond's own liking for the contrasts of "requiem and celebration" and, together with *misère*, adds to the mediaeval aura alluded to in the "book of hours". Ormond, unlike Glenys, was not a birdwatcher, but he was interested in the science of things and it was satisfying when he found that observations in *The Times*'s science report on blackbird behaviour seemed to chime with his poem.

Certain Questions for Monsieur Renoir
Anglo-Welsh Review Vol. 22, No. 50, Autumn 1973
As aide-memoire for a reading, Ormond noted Théophile Gautier's poem '*Symphonie en Blanc Majeur*', adding that he had considered the title 'Blue Major' for the poem. It was inspired by Pierre-Auguste Renoir's '*La Parisienne*' – known as 'The Blue Lady' and exhibited at the first Impressionist exhibition

of 1874 – hanging in the National Museum of Wales in Cardiff. Renoir's sitter had been the actress Madame Henriette Henriot, whom he frequently used as a model. Ormond made her a seamstress, admitting to Richard Poole (*op.cit.*) that he'd probably been seduced by the idea of putting together the words "midnight" and "midinette", the Parisian name for a seamstress. In the same conversation, he said: "I've never tried to hide the fact at poetry readings that it took me some time to assemble the vocabulary of blue for that poem. I think it probably occupied me for maybe seven or eight months.... [but] in the end came quite quickly ... in a single day. I got the first draft done from colour-notes and associations of blue which ran into many pages." The line "humanly on the verge of the ceramic" refers to the Meissen and Dresden figurines where ladies' flounced skirts were faithfully rendered in porcelain.

The Birth of Venus at Aberystwyth

Anglo-Welsh Review (*ibid.*) and in the P.E.N. Anthology, *New Poems 74* (ed. Stewart Conn).

This poem was begun when Ormond was in Aberystwyth in 1973 to discuss the making of the film *One Man in his Time*: a portrait of W.J.G. Beynon (his cousin Granville, professor of physics at the university, who had been made a Fellow of the Royal Society earlier that year). The idea of Botticelli's Roman goddess rising from the waves and exciting the dolphins in the waters of Cardigan Bay is a typically playful conceit: no matter that the Aberystwyth sea is mostly cold and inhospitable by comparison with the Mediterranean, dolphins do indeed swim in the vicinity and sighting them had begun the process of association. In a note for a reading, Ormond had written "Jimmy Leach and the Organolians": this dance band was known for playing on radio's 'Music While You Work' and they did summer seasons at Aberystwyth, 1973 included. Leach himself was the organist and his line-up included a violinist, presumably wearing tartan.

Letter to a Geologist

Anglo-Welsh Review (*ibid.*)

Wynn Williams was always the first port of call in any queries Ormond had about the geography and geology of Wales. Moreover, Ormond liked him to confirm that what he wrote - whether in verse or in film commentaries - stood up credibly. By the same token, Williams could enthuse to Ormond about geological matters, and the coral specimen he gave him was symbolic of their enduring friendship. Williams lived in Gwern y Mynydd, Flintshire and, as the poem makes clear, Ormond wished him back south. That didn't happen; though, as Glenys remembered with poignancy in her brief memoir written for *Poetry Wales* 27/3, (1990), Williams joined her in singing lullabies as Ormond lay dying.

Notes to a Suicide

Poetry Wales 22/3, Spring 1987

This poem commemorates the poet B.S. Johnson, who committed suicide in November, 1973. Bryan Johnson and Ormond had met at Gregynog in 1970, when Johnson was in residence there as University of Wales Arts Fellow; he inscribed his book of Poems (Constable, 1964) "to John Ormond with respect". When Johnson was poetry editor of *Transatlantic Review*, he asked to include Ormond's work in a special edition of Anglo-Welsh poetry and it was he who, in his capacity as editor, had originally chosen Ormond to appear along with Emyr Humphries and John Tripp in the *Penguin Modern Poets 27*, a volume whose appearance was then long delayed following Johnson's death. The reference to the aerial shot of a man in the sea is to the end of the film, *Fat Man on a Beach*, which Johnson had made earlier in 1973, when he himself waded into the sea at Porth Ceiriad, in North Wales.

Design for a Quilt
Aquarius 5, 1975.
Invited by Eddie Linden, founder of the journal *Aquarius*, to be guest-editor of this Welsh issue, Ormond was encouraged by Linden to include work of his own. The poem then appeared the following year in *Poems 76*, edited by Glyn Jones. It had its inspiration in an exhibition, entitled 'Twelve Masterpieces of American Quilts', which the Ormonds saw in New York during their 1974 visit. Ormond only went to the exhibition under duress but, given the resulting poem, Glenys was pleased to point to her good instinct in such matters. When introducing it as a love-poem in the BBC Radio 3 programme, 'The Living Poet' (broadcast on 22 January 1982), Ormond said: "One [of the quilts] had a great tree embroidered on it, but a tree with precious few leaves, I thought; too few to keep the Babes in the Wood warm when they got lost again. This thought and the notion of warmth and cold stayed with me and became a prime image when I imagined a lover commissioning a present for his girl and describing to the quiltmaker his design." Ormond sometimes took a slightly cynical view of the business of others' interpretation of poems: when an examination board set 'Design for a Quilt' as the poem for analysis, he liked pointing out that he would not have been able to answer the questions they set.

A Lost Word
Poetry Supplement, compiled by Dannie Abse for the Poetry Book Society, 1975
In 'The Living Poet', Ormond prefaced his reading of this poem thus: "The next piece needs no more introduction than to say that we all feel from time to time that the world we live in and the whole cosmic context of it has no right to be quite so mysterious, and yet that occasionally it seems that some meaning is nearly at hand for the touching."

Captive Unicorn
Anglo-Welsh Review, Vol. 26, No. 59, Autumn 1977
The poem takes its title from a tapestry entitled 'The Unicorn in Captivity and No longer Dead', seventh and last in the series called 'The Hunt of the Unicorn' hanging in the Cloisters of the Metropolitan Museum of Art, New York. The Ormonds had seen them there in the autumn of 1974. It goes without saying that tapestry had hitherto not been an interest of Ormond's: Glenys remembered him objecting to being dragged to see this exhibition too, but the visit evidently made its mark. The Unicorn tapestries are Flemish in origin and date from the end of the 15th into the 16th century; their images signify earthly love and fruitful marriage, inviting both Christian and pagan interpretations. The seventh represents the finale to the allegorical love hunt described in medieval poetry, where the unicorn, having been hunted to death, is restored to life. Ormond's poem is faithful to the image depicted in the tapestry: the unicorn is seen resting within

a circular wooden enclosure or palisade, collared and chained to a pomegranate tree, emblematic of being secured at last by his bride. This style of tapestry is called *millefleurs* and, in these particular examples, the background apparently affords more accurate depictions of the flowers than are found in botanists' records of the time. Glenys had studied botany so she could recognise many of the flowers; Ormond's curiosity was aroused by their names and the tapestry's symbolic associations. The horn as periscope is a characteristic Ormond quirk.

Night in a Hundred
Poetry Supplement, compiled by Dannie Abse for the Poetry Book Society, 1975. The myth of Cantre'r Gwaelod, literally Lowland of the Hundred and usually located in Cardigan Bay off the West Wales coast, tells of an ancient kingdom submerged by the sea. Its church bells are said to ring out to warn of times of danger. The town of Aberdyfi is closely associated with the legend of the drowned Cantre'r Gwaelod, hence the well-known song – 'Clychau Aberdyfi' (The Bells of Aberdyfi) – to which Ormond alludes in the final line. As well as relating to the legends of Dunwich, off the Suffolk coast, and Lyonesse, off the coast of Cornwall, Cantre'r Gwaelod has another Celtic equivalent in the sunken cathedral city of Ys, off the coast of Brittany, a particular inspiration for the painter Ceri Richards. His many works based on the legend also drew on the soundscape of Debussy's 1910 prelude for piano, *La Cathédrale Engloutie*, with its invocation of Ys's chiming bells. In Ormond's film portrait of Richards, the painter explained the fascination and himself played part of the prelude. The introduction which Ormond wrote for the National Museum's Ceri Richards retrospective in Cardiff in 1973 seems to have brought to mind their discussion of the parallel legends and provided the impulse for the poem.

An Ending
New Poems, 1975, P.E.N. (ed. Patricia Beer, Hutchinson)
Ormond originally considered the title 'Noli me Tangere' for this poem, "Touch me not", the words which in St. John's gospel were spoken by Jesus to Mary Magdalene when she recognised him after the resurrection. Ormond's mother Elsie had died on the 8th of December, 1965, but the memory of the night of her death, and of his vigil with her body, haunted him for the best part of a decade before emerging in poetic form. A partial draft is dated June 29, 1974. While other poems dealing with his leave-taking of the house and its many associations came to fruition much earlier, it was to some extent Ormond's experience of being a grandfather (his grandson Ceri was born on the first day of 1973) that led to further reflection on his own early life, to that of his mother and, with it, her death.

Note Found on a Mantelpiece
Anglo-Welsh Review, Vol. 25, No. 56, Spring 1976
Amended by the time of its appearance in *Selected Poems*, this poem's title was simply 'Note on a Mantelpiece' when first published. It was included as such on the October page of a Poem Calendar for Wales 1977. Ormond later used that page on his calendar to write a note for his friend and colleague Simon Horwood arriving to house-sit: "for Simon to give him a welcome & a gratitude from J.O. 20 September 1978 N.B. And don't forget to drain the leaking geyser!!!"

Horwood found it propped on the mantelpiece.

Homing Pigeons
Times Literary Supplement, in an edition for St David's Day, March 4, 1977
In the days when Dunvant still had a working railway-station, Ormond would see racing pigeons packed into their small baskets waiting to be transported to places from where they would be released to fly home. Some years after the poem's publication, Ormond was delighted to learn of scientists' discovery that magnetoreceptors in the beak were a conditioning factor in bird navigation and in pigeon-homing in particular. He felt it suitable validation of his instinctive, though at the time entirely speculative, use of the word "lode-stone" (the mineral magnetite, with its naturally magnetic properties). It had also pleased him to put the word "beguilement" together with "shepherds", since the Welsh word for shepherd is bugail, (like "*beguile*" but with its first syllable accented). While Ormond was undoubtedly influenced by the sounds of the Welsh language – he heard it all around him in Dunvant, among his fellow-students at university and within his own family – this is a rare example of bilingual wordplay.

Patagonian Portrait
Planet 36, February/March 1977
Appearing in *Planet* under the title In Certain Lights : Two extracts from a work in progress, and following a prose piece called *Bad Light Stops Play* [see also later note for 'Ode to Winston Place'], this poem is slightly surprising for appearing fifteen years after Ormond's visit to Patagonia. It had been Ormond's suggestion that his friend, the artist Kyffin Williams, apply for a Churchill fellowship to go and paint there, which he had done in 1968. Williams was a frequent visitor to the Ormonds' home over the years; around the time the second film portrait of Williams – this one in colour – was being discussed, it seems that the conversations, which often turned to their respective perceptions of Patagonia, triggered a memory for Ormond and, with it, this poem.

Landscape in Dyfed
Spring Collection, Mandeville Press, 1977
The Mandeville Press, run by poet Peter Scupham with John Mole and based in Hitchin in Hertfordshire, produced very beautiful limited editions of poetry. Ormond's great respect for the craftsmanship and quality of these publications meant that Scupham's request for a poem met with an immediate response. 'Landscape in Dyfed' was the first of this series of seventeen poems by different authors. Ormond was still at college when he first encountered the work of Graham Sutherland (1903-1980) in the latter's *Welsh Sketchbook* (Horizon, April 1942), and in his illustrations for David Gascoyne's volume of *Poems 1937-1942* (Poetry London editions, 1943). The two men would meet over thirty years later when, in 1976, Kathleen and Graham Sutherland donated a major body of work to the Welsh nation in acknowledgement of the influence of the West Wales landscape on the artist's creative output. The collection was housed in the Sutherland Gallery at Picton Castle in Pembrokeshire though, much later, was transferred to St. David's. Ormond made a film portrait of Sutherland to mark the gallery's opening and this saw the beginning of a close friendship. Sutherland died on 17 February 1980. It had been his wish that Ormond speak at his memorial service

and this poem formed part of that address. In Ormond's own copy of the *Spring Collection*, noting that the poem was written as homage to the painter, he wrote: "That there is something very special about the landscape of Pembrokeshire there has never been any doubt. In legend, Dyfed was the kingdom beyond the gate of life, a region of darkness and of enchantment. In an essay I read in 1942, Graham Sutherland [said that] 'the landscape seems poised on the brink of some drama'". Noting Sutherland's imagery, he added: "The otherness of Pembrokeshire, the qualities that were once magical and for some [they] are so still." In his 1983 lecture, *In Place of an Empty Heaven: the Poetry of Wallace Stevens*, Ormond quoted from Stevens's 'Adagia': "Poetry is a search for the inexplicable. Literature is not based on life but on propositions about life, of which this [following] is one." He continued: "Stevens's notion, that must help to make life bearable, [...] is that our perceptions and, in the Kantian sense, our apprehension of the world, suggest to us that there is a kind of parallel reality which we, out of our imagination, create. This imagined reality (and the painter Graham Sutherland based all his landscape work upon the same belief) is the true one, or at least a truer one. But, even so, it cannot be explained."

Tune for a Celestial Musician
Anglo-Welsh Review, Vol. 26, No. 59, Autumn 1977
The line "Play it, Sam" from the 1942 film *Casablanca* has long since evolved into the phrase "Play it again, Sam", hence Ormond's "Play it again, Sam angel, play it again". Curiously, in an early draft for the poem, the line appears as "Play it again, Apsaras." The Apsaras, usually translated as celestial nymphs or maidens, are the female spirits of the clouds and waters in Hindu and Buddhist mythology, ethereal beings, comparable to angels. Dannie Abse chose this poem to read at Ormond's memorial service.

The Gift
Mandeville Press Dragoncard, 1978
Ormond made this the introductory poem of his *Selected Poems*, a symbolic and emblematic positioning he was happy to repeat in the Gregynog Press's *Cathedral Builders*. A first draft of 'The Gift' exists in a tiny, green-covered, note-book in which Ormond recorded a conversation with his friend and former philosophy lecturer Rush Rhees, including references to Rhees's friend, Ludwig Wittgenstein. The notes are dated Good Friday, 1978. After the poem's appearance in the Mandeville Dragoncard series, Ormond also had 'The Gift' printed to send as Christmas cards: on the front, he did a pen-and-ink drawing of flames of fire and flower-like whorls which he hand-coloured individually. In this earliest form, the third line read "As pointless to ask for truth in pictures". The following Christmas, Ormond sent friends the Mandeville's 1979 printing of his poem 'Year In, Year Out', also sending some as New Year greetings. He coupled as keepsakes a copy each of 'The Gift' and 'Year In, Year Out' and, on the reverse of the latter, is the single word 'epiphanies' – in his hand and in ink – suggesting that the word came to him by association when writing his Christmas greetings. By the time 'The Gift' appeared in *Poetry Wales* in 1980, he had made the revision, replacing "pictures" with "epiphanies". Ormond's hope had always been for the revelatory message yet, here, there is acceptance, apparently for the first

time, that that would never come. In Radio 3's 'The Living Poet', following his reading of the poem 'As it Happens' with its final line "There being no alternative to being", Ormond added: "That's not a thought that used to haunt me but, as I've got older, it has rather. That the alternative to having the joys and sorrows of one's life would have been not to have had them, never to have been born. Of course, if you pursue that notion it leads to the idea that the whole of life and the world and everything in space is one boundless miracle. In 'The Gift' [which he went on to read] I abandon hopes of trying to fathom the mystery."

Where Else?
Poetry Wales 16/2, Autumn 1980

As it Happens
The Living Poet, BBC Radio 3, January 1982

Decades had gone by since Ormond had attempted to paint a self-portrait (his friend Bill Price remembers seeing a well-executed one in a school exhibition), but the questioning gaze into the mirror which he was unwilling to dwell on in 'A Lost Word' is held for longer here and, as in 'The Gift', the conclusion he reaches is altogether more celebratory.

Year In, Year Out
Mandeville Press Dragoncard, 1979

For the Mandeville's postcard-format Dragoncard, the poem appeared as a single stanza. In a piece written around the same time for the magazine of the celebrated Dunvant Male Choir, Ormond included two stanzas of the poem, explaining that it had sprung from a memory of the choir, dating from his late teens. Then known as the Dunvant Excelsior Male Voice Party, their custom was to go carolling on New Year's Eve. "We sang around the village," he wrote, "and walked in the dark, even to the most distant farms where, if the evidence of past rewards was anything to go by, we would receive such reimbursements as would justify the hard slog of our midnight minstrelsy. We would have sung 'A Happy New Year to you all, in this house both great and small!' and 'Blwyddyn Newydd Dda i Chwi, Ac i bawb sydd yn y tŷ' many times before, hoarse and weary, we could get home to tumble into our cold beds." They sometimes collected as much as ten pounds – as Ormond put it, "a nearly astronomical sum, the equivalent of a working man's wages for perhaps five weeks" – the money going to the Sunday School to help pay for the books given to children at Christmas.

Among Friends
Strict Seasons, Starwheel Press, 1980

The Starwheel Press, run by poet George Szirtes and his artist wife, Clarissa Upchurch, published this in their portfolio of five poems, taking the title from the last line of Ormond's poem. Each had its own etching, with 'Among Friends' illustrated by Mary Norman.

Cat's Cradles
Poetry Wales 16/2, Autumn 1980

Ormond told Richard Poole (*op.cit.*) that 'Cat's Cradles' had begun as a villanelle, betrayed in the tercets and partial repetitions of rhymes. But he said he'd "moved away from the tight structure of the villanelle to something more fluid, to give the hand-to-hand movement in the cat's cradle". "Popinjay" was very much a term of endearment in the Ormond household, especially used for children, with no pejorative connotation at all.

There There, Then

Poetry Wales (ibid.)

Ormond was by this stage a devoted grandfather, a surprisingly reassuring figure not unused to consoling small children, but his experience is translated into more reflective vein here. In 'The Living Poet', Ormond prefaced his reading of the poem with the following words: "Do you remember falling as a child and being picked up? You know how it is when you pick up some little one when it has taken a great tumble and after the screams it holds its breath and it feels as though the child is never going to let go its breath again?" The title reflects a fundamentally Welsh inflection of language, since the rhythm of "There There, Then", imitates the consoling rhythm and emphasis of the Welsh phrase " 'Na ni, te", literally "There we are, then,".

Several Episodes Reported with No Offence Meant to God

Arcade No.1, October 31st, 1980

Arcade magazine, edited by John Osmond (their names were sometimes confused over the years) and dedicated to covering politics, literature and the arts, appeared fortnightly from October 1980 to March, 1982. Ormond's sequence of poems took a whole page of the inaugural publication, while the following number featured a profile of him by David (Dai) Smith. The title as it appeared in *Arcade* was 'Several Episodes Reported with No Offence to God', the word "Meant" added for *Selected Poems*. Other minimal changes included removing the indefinite article in the title of 'Song of Anti-Matter'. A manuscript of the latter is dated Tuesday 21st August [1979].

Ode To Winston Place

This last poem of the sequence – not obvious Ormond territory – relates specifically to the end of the prose piece he called 'Bad Light Stops Play', published in *Planet* 36, February/March 1977. Not quite amounting to a short story, the piece tells of a Dunvant cricket-team game where bad light, bad lenses and bad vision conspire in a batsman's demise; Ormond suggested that an umpire with a sense of compassion would have given a no-ball. He added: "I think of Winston Place, former Lancashire cricketer [1914-2002], decorous at the crease, who upon retirement became an umpire. But he retired from this task too, finding it obnoxious to give people out. God in your utmost green hiding-place, when bad light stops play let Winston Place be a lesson to you." The ensuing brief ode varied this only slightly, with "green" lost altogether. The idea that the great umpire in the sky might profitably learn from the humility and grace of a mere mortal has the mark of the lightly philosophical banter Ormond enjoyed sharing with Place's fellow Lancastrian and cricket-fan, the writer Peter Tinniswood, who went on to quote from the ode in his television series *I Didn't Know You Cared*. 'Bad Light Stops Play' appeared together with the poem Patagonian Portrait (*q.v.*). This rather curious pairing came under the general title 'In Certain Lights', a phrase Ormond had used at the opening of his poem 'A Lost Word'. It would be mooted as the title for an autobiographical work which never actually appeared.

Of Exits

Poems for Shakespeare 9 (edited and with an Introduction by Dannie Abse) Globe Playhouse Publications, London 1981

The publication was one of a series of anthologies issued by the Globe Theatre. The actor Norman Wynne, affectionately maligned here along with Richard Burbage, was a Welshman whom Ormond had indeed known from radio productions in Swansea. During his time at the *South Wales Evening Post*, Ormond had tried his hand at playwriting and Wynne took part in his play, *Man in Darkness*, broadcast by the BBC in 1952. Wynne became a familiar face in television dramas in the 60s. He died in 1968.

Castiglion Fiorentino

The Living Poet, BBC Radio 3, January 1982

When Ormond returned to Italy in 1981, he wanted to search out a vista, the memory of which had tantalised him since first sighting it in 1963. Writing in *Letter from Tuscany* (*op.cit.*), he recalled filming "a small arcade of pillars and arched windows that looked down over a meadow with a hillside of vines climbing above it". Yet, as the poem makes clear, he was not entirely convinced that Castiglion Fiorentino would prove to be the right place. This Arcadian vision was in fact the town's Logge del Vasari: a single-storied loggia with a not 8- but 9-arched and pillared facade and, on the opposite side, a three-arched opening overlooking the Val di Chio below. Its construction was begun in 1513 and the architect Giorgio Vasari only became involved when the loggia was being restored fifty years later, after which it was given his name. If Ormond's return visit was not exactly the heart-stopping affair of memory, it was because a football stadium had been built in the intervening years, spoiling the view, but mentioning that would also have spoiled the poem.

Elsewhere

The Living Poet, BBC Radio 3, January 1982

An early draft of this poem is dated 17 February 1978, with a later draft signed, ok JO July 30 /1981 [Cortona]; a note on it suggests that the idea came to him when staying in Winchester in the house of the painter, John Elwyn. Elwyn was a close friend of poet Glyn Jones and the fact that all three had been pacifists and conscientious objectors gave them a particular bond. In 'The Living Poet' broadcast, Ormond introduced the poem by saying that, while he couched it in a domestic guise, its central thought "really derives from that notion in a fragment of Heraclitus which says that in sleep and death we recede into our private selves, that the only morality is between the living, the shared *logos* in the waking world". He supposed the poem's last lines to be "a hint of the darker side of my life, an indication of my need for a sense of order and this is clearly denied one who has lost the reassurances of a formal faith. But of course this doesn't mean that I don't, every day, wonder."

For Glenys

The Living Poet, BBC Radio 3, January 1982

A manuscript with the poem more or less fixed (typed, with changes in blue pencil) is dated Cortona, Tues July 14, 1981; the final corrected version, typed again once back home, confirms that date. It was one of the small handful of poems Ormond wrote or began in Cortona that summer, having immediately sensed that he would be able to write there.

Right Time
Selected Poems, 1987
A copy of Right Time is dated 1982. The clock in this poem had belonged to Ormond's maternal grandfather, commemorated for his apple-tree and finally also in 'Family Matters'. The phrase "and truly my grandfather's clock" is a nod to Henry Clay Work's old American song, whose huge popularity resulted in what had previously been known as a standing clock (also a coffin clock) acquiring its more familiar name. Ormond's lines describe exactly the clock he inherited: painted on enamel, the four-part image around the clock-face depicted idyllic cottages facing the seashore, whose sands allude to those of the hour-glass, used since medieval times to measure time. It is usually a clock's regular ticking that is said to be good company, but a note suggests that in the last lines Ormond was again influenced by Heraclitus and his saying "Silence, healing", with the silent clock effecting a kind of reconciliation with his long-dead grandfather and a relationship which had clearly perplexed him.

Note from Cortona
Selected Poems, 1987
This poem was originally entitled 'Letter from Cortona' and a draft manuscript, only marginally different, is dated September 21, 1983, making it another anniversary poem for Glenys. The stone table was at the bar *Il Belvedere*, over the mountain in nearby Torreone, where the old couple who owned it always welcomed Ormond warmly. It was they who one day, speculating as to his profession, thought he must be a brain surgeon, whereupon he surprised himself by feeling wholly comfortable in responding '*Sono un poeta*', familiar to Italians from Rodolfo's description of himself to Mimi in Puccini's opera *La Bohème*. The old couple were delighted. The poem's original title would later prompt that of Ormond's *Letter from Tuscany* (*op.cit.*). This piece, documenting the start of his relationship with Italy, and Cortona in particular, took the form of a letter to his friend Clive (Ginty) Morris. They did actually correspond, though that particular missive was merely a device.

Storm
Selected Poems, 1989
A letter to Ginty Morris written from Cortona on 29 May, 1986, recounts: "two days of thunderstorms, knockouts [electricity] yesterday, today blackmailing rumbles to keep me in. I've got a piece of something written about the storm:

Lightning, turn mirrors to the wall
Lest it stop to look at itself, then kill.

First shunting of heavy trucks in the sky,
Then the first blast furnaces bursting wide open;

Four million old iron bedsteads thrown out
(Where will the Roman gods sleep to-night?)

Someone has broken all the commandments,
The sound of all the saints' bones fracturing,"

Then, following paeans of praise for the quality and colour of Italian vegetables, he returns to the storm in prose: "The storm rumbles; in the distance celestial floor-boards are being ripped up, a million tons of best anthracite being poured down tin cellars ... And the rain comes rifling in through the open window. The plain, 1600 feet below (latest check) is blurred. The storm comes straight across from the south-west (honest) spilling rain for three feet into the room. [closes window]." The fourth couplet quoted above didn't make it into the poem's final version, but some of the prose description did. Other details are more personal: the cupboard under the stairs relates to his childhood home in Dunvant, while the tin cellars were like that of the house in Conway Road where the sound of coal being delivered down the cellar-shute could be thunderous. Glenys was adept at cracking all manner of nuts – walnuts a favourite – and it infuriated her husband that she disdained any nutcracker, preferring to keep a large stone for the purpose.

Evening in the Square
Selected Poems, 1987

It was on the mountainside above Cortona that Ormond first became aware of the hustling of hundreds of swifts overhead, sometimes so close he could "feel the slipstream of their flight" and, in a postcard dated July 1983, he records their nesting in the tiles above his room. In his *Letter from Tuscany* (*op.cit.*), Ormond mentions this poem as being written in the summer of 1986. Its title was perhaps his most nostalgic linking of Dunvant with Cortona. In Dunvant, the square – though not really a square at all – was central to life in the village; the small medieval city of Cortona could hardly have been more different, but its *piazze* were equally the hub of the community, Piazza Signorelli, named for Cortona's most celebrated painter, being his favourite. Ormond's references to stitching and needlework in this and other poems are affectionate homage to his mother. She loved to embroider as well as doing the darning, habitually necessary in their predominantly male household.

Waiting in the Garden
Poetry Wales 22/3, Spring 1987

The seed of this poem was sown during a visit Ormond and his wife made to Spain in September, 1977: jottings in manuscript and notes of prospective titles refer to 'Garden in Toledo' and also to 'Evening Garden'. The Toledo garden in question was formerly that of a cardinal's palace, later a hotel, and their stay was a wedding anniversary holiday. Seeing El Greco's painting *The Assumption* at the Museo de Santa Cruz seems also to have been significant, and the Baroque altar-piece, known as *El Transparente*, in Toledo Cathedral even more so. In the cathedral's ambulatory are two openings - one a large skylight and another in the back of the altarpiece itself – which allow shafts of sunlight to enter; the two are connected by sculptures of angels and saints, with Christ on a bank of clouds and biblical figures arranged so as to appear to be tumbling down into the cathedral. These seeds remained dormant until further inspiration came in Cortona, at the Giardini dei Tigli, under whose linden-trees Ormond loved to sit. A starred note in the blank space of an advertisement in his copy of *Private Eye*, dated October 1984, is a reminder to "Get on with the Toledo Transparente poem". There, too, are the words "trampling the rhubarb", underlining that, in the end, the garden in the poem is undoubtedly the one created by Glenys in Conway Road, resplendent with trees and flowering shrubs, as well as rhubarb. It is a slight irony that it took Ormond much foreign travel to appreciate the green beauty of the garden at home and to find it conducive to thinking and writing though, as he acknowledges in the phrase "this lady's garden", it was very much Glenys's domain. He would teasingly refer to her as "Capability Roderick" and, in the poem, his disinclination to be spirited away from it - no matter how enticing the possibility of having the great mystery of life revealed - is another late gesture of love. The angels on their motorbikes relate specifically to Spain and Italy, where the custom is for death announcements, as well as being published in newspapers, to be pasted on walls, in the manner of fly-posting. The notices are writ large, the print starkly black on the background of white. On Spanish and Italian sojourns, the Ormonds were moved to see that many of the dead were young men killed in motorcycle accidents, hence their being memorialised here as God's patrolmen and messengers on flying visits. But, as Ormond's early poem 'The Angels in the Air' among others underlines, the notion of angels had long intrigued him, as had the idea that life – if one were patient and listened carefully enough – might at some point reveal its deeper meaning. Ormond's quest for the great revelatory message was never entirely abandoned, as 'The Gift' and other poems might have it, but this poem is further suggestion that he was again reconciling himself to the fact that not even angels would have a better answer than the one offered by being alive to life in the present.

Illuminations of the Letter O

Selected Poems, 1987

The notion of a scene depicted within the perimeter of the letter O seems to relate to images by the Italian artist, Liberale da Verona (1441-1526), from illuminated pages he painted early in his career for a choir-book of *Graduali e Antifonari*, which the Ormonds saw when visiting the Libreria Piccolomini in Siena Cathedral. A poster they bought there is a reproduction of one of its pages, its neumes – notes in medieval script on four-line staves – a setting of the Latin words *Circumdederunt me gemitus mortis*. The music has an elaborate border of flowers, leaves and plumes, with the attribution *Opus Liberalis Veronesis*. The top left-hand quarter of the page is filled with an equally ornately decorated letter O which frames an illustration of the parable of the vineyard (*Parabola dei Vignaioli*). Liberale illustrated other parables, including that of the Good Samaritan, the Beam and the Mote, and the parable of the Lost Sheep, and it is the latter which Ormond seems to have chosen to touch on in the poem, with his reference to the shepherd prodding around in the snow. The parable's message is that one repenting sinner to whom the kingdom of heaven will be opened is more welcome than the ninety-nine who are righteous; yet Ormond's play on the letter O and zero and nothing, underlining the nothing at its heart, suggests a reflection on the absence of faith. As such, it would represent quite a firm rejection of the Christian teaching and thus of any possibility of repentance. The loss of his early religious conviction was a gradual process, and it may be that working on the film portrait *R.S. Thomas: Priest and Poet*, a decade and a half earlier, and their discussions on the nature of faith and doctrine, was a time which permitted Ormond to acknowledge without angst his own journey from Christian pacifism to the doubting Thomas he had become. Despite the depth of their discussions and the fact that each remembered the other with apparent affection in later years, R.S.'s natural austerity was not Ormond's style and they never became close friends. Ormond's affinity for the poet Wallace Stevens suggests that the allusion in the title to Stevens's mock-epic 'The Comedian as the Letter C' was not unconscious.

Turning
Selected Poems, 1987
This is set in the same Conway Road garden, where Glenys loudly clapped away the magpies that terrorised the small birds and where a sparrow-hawk had once dropped down into the apple-tree to take away a blackbird in its talons. Winter aconite did flower there in February but, while the "Italianate gesture" was one Ormond himself often used to point up a defining word or phrase in conversation, his botany is deficient here. Winter aconite (*Eranthis hyemalis*) has six petals, not five.

Soliloquy of a Secret Policeman
Poets against Apartheid, Welsh Anti-Apartheid Movement, 1986
In conversation with Richard Poole (*op.cit.*), Ormond explained that he had promised a poem for this anthology, though it had only come to him within a day or two of the deadline. "Going to bed late one night, 3 o'clock in the morning, I suddenly got the title as a donée as my head hit the pillow. I had to get up and go to my workroom. I wrote a few lines and then went back to bed, thinking, 'Well, something has started. Let's see if it works out.' But then I had to get up again within a matter of minutes. And it came tumbling out...but it wasn't my voice. I showed it to some of my friends and they were horrified to find this terror on the page... Yes, there is a domestic note, but it is true, isn't it, that the people who perpetrate this kind of awfulness are people with homes, children. If I'm pleased about anything in the piece it's the last couple of lines, about teaching the children to count on the gun." Ormond read this at a benefit night for Friends of the Earth Cymru in 1986, in the Lion's Den cellar bar of the Great Western pub in Cardiff. Robert Minhinnick in his piece on Ormond in *Poetry Wales* 27/3, December 1990, wrote that he "stilled the crush" with this poem.

Tuscan Cypresses
Selected Poems, 1987
Ormond had been fascinated by cypress trees when he first went to Italy in 1963 but, in 'Castiglion Fiorentino', the poem he wrote on returning there in the early 80s, his phrase "the never-sleeping of cypresses" symbolically spanning the end of the third and beginning of the fourth stanza, is perhaps a first clue that this iconic feature of the Tuscan landscape would become a major focus. Ormond

would certainly have known of D.H. Lawrence's poem 'Cypresses', and his youthful admiration for Lawrence's 'Giorno dei Morti' with its opening line "Along the avenue of cypresses" has already been noted. He began to toy with the subject early in 1984 during the winter sojourn just outside Florence, where the garden of Villa Clemente had many such noble trees, and the idea continued to ferment for a good while longer. In his *Letter from Tuscany* (*op.cit.*) dated July, 1986, Ormond wrote: "This year has seen me write a long piece I've called Tuscan Cypresses". Later, in conversation with Richard Poole (*op.cit.*), he spoke of it as a poem which had come with "a sense of rhythm swelling and finding the notes, the words, when the rhythm has somehow established itself…Somehow I got the long extended-line rhythm before I began to work out in it my obsession with these trees that had haunted me from the very first time I saw them… Curiously – and I find it difficult to believe now – I got a version of that poem done in a week, carrying it around in the backside pocket of my trousers, and working on it over a glass of wine somewhere, over a meal, on walks, stopping on a rock to write a couple of lines…"

Agnolo di Tura, sometimes Angelo di Tura (detto il Grasso) ["called the Fat"] was a 14th century chronicler, though perhaps only the copyist, who recorded in the *Cronica Sanese* two decades of events in Siena, including burying five of his own children who died of the plague in 1348. Di Tura was an artisan shoemaker, which may explain Ormond's alighting on the name, since his own father had been a master shoemaker.

Saint Teresa's Drum
New Welsh Review 5, Vol. II, No.1, Summer 1989

Spanish saint and mystic Teresa of Avila was a Carmelite nun, celebrated for her writing about the contemplative life. The poem had its origins in a visit to Avila's Convento de San José, founded by Teresa, where Ormond learned about her experience of illness and of the ecstatic visions. At the convent's museum, he saw objects thought to have belonged to her: among them were castanets and the tambourine-like drum to which Teresa is said to have danced on Christmas morning. An early draft of the poem, entitled 'Santa Teresa's Drum', began: "In her dark garden in Avila/ I stood, feeling nothing. Overgrown/ With velvet moss, in shade that could not permit [progeniture?] (Ormond's brackets and question-mark) /It was a perfect tragic theatre…" Those rejected lines, written in the first person, stand in marked contrast to the way the legend of the drum would later seize his imagination (a sheet of lists, c.1979/80, includes 'The Drum, ta-rum, ta-rum' circled for emphasis), leading him to explore the notion that Teresa's deliriously ecstatic state was caused by eating blessed, but toxic, bread at communion. Ergot poisoning, known as St. Anthony's Fire, occurs when cereal grain is infected by the deadly fungus, *Claviceps purpurea*. The lunge of the angel's spear is reference to Teresa's own description (in *The Life of St. Teresa of Avila* by Teresa herself) of an angel carrying a fire-tipped spear piercing her heart repeatedly and sending her into a state of spiritual raptures. "The sweetness caused by this intense pain is so extreme that one cannot possibly wish it to cease, nor is one's soul then content with anything but God." Bernini's sculpture *The Ecstasy of St. Teresa* is a representation of this.

Blue Bath-gown
New Welsh Review 5 (ibid.)
An early draft can be dated to September 1987, with another manuscript dated October 19, 1988, and even more precisely 5.35-5.50. The only difference between early and final versions is in line-breaks. The blue bath-gown – with its oblique allusion to the A.A.Milne poem, 'Vespers' and Nanny's beautiful blue dressing-gown – was Glenys's pale blue towelling bath-robe.

Family Matters
Poetry Book Society Anthology I (ed. Fraser Steel, Hutchinson) 1990
Garan's daughter Katherine, known as Katie, was born on April 3, 1989, Ormond's 66th birthday. He began the poem then, returning to it again to inscribe and frame it as a gift for her first birthday. It was a joyous day. No-one could have known that, but one month and a day later, he would be dead. Yet, the conscious invoking of his grandfather and the cyclic nature of life makes it clear that Ormond himself was probably all too aware of his own mortality.

Television Films by John Ormond

A Sort of Welcome to Spring. (1959).

Borrowed Pasture. 1960).

Once there was a time. (1961).

The Desert and the Dream. (1962)

Y Gymru Bell: taith i Batagonia. [series of 3, producer Nan Davies] (1962)

From a town in Tuscany. (1963)

Return Journey: The Story of Dylan Thomas's Return Journey to Swansea. (1964)

Songs in a Strange Land: a study of three religious communities in Cardiff. (1964).

The Mormons: from Merthyr to Salt Lake City. (1965)

Alone in a Boat. (1965)

Troubled Waters: the challenge to rivers and fishermen in West Wales. (1965)

My Time Again: Richard Burton. (1966)

My Time Again: Harry Secombe.

Just Look Again: a series of five films. (1966)

Under a Bright Heaven: A film portrait of Vernon Watkins. (1966)

Horizons Hung in Air: the artist Kyffin Williams. [B&W] (1966)

Madawaska Valley (for the National Film Board of Canada). (1967)

Piano with Many Strings: the art of Ceri Richards. (1967)

Music in Midsummer: The Llangollen Eisteddfod. (1968)

A Bronze Mask: a film in elegy for Dylan Thomas. (1969)

The Ancient Kingdoms: a film to mark the Investiture of the Prince of Wales. (1969)

The Fragile Universe: Alun Lewis, the soldier-poet. (1969)

Private View of Art and Artists in Wales: Leslie Norris. (1970)

Robert Graves. (1970)

R.S. Thomas: Priest and Poet. (1971)

The Land Remembers: the history of Wales from ancient times (2 series of 13 half-hour films, 1971-73 & 1974-75).

The Travellers: the artist John 'Warwick' Smith, set in 1797 (1973).

A Day Eleven Years Long: a film portrait of painter Josef Herman (1975).

One Man in his Time: W.J.G. Beynon, F.R.S. (1975)

The Life and Death of Picture Post. (1977)

Sutherland in Wales. (1977)

Fortissimo Jones: a portrait of the composer Daniel Jones. (1978)
A Land against the Light: Kyffin Williams. [colour] (1978)
The Colliers' Crusade: a series of five films tracing the contribution of Welsh miners to the Republican cause during the Spanish Civil War. (1979)
Poems in their Place: seven films tracing associations of landscape and verse. (1980-81)
I Sing to You Strangers: a film biography of Dylan Thomas (1982)

Ormond wrote the commentaries for all his films, he also wrote commentaries for:
Heart of Scotland (director: Lawrence Henson, 1961)
Far from Paradise (a series of 7 50-minute films, director: Brian Turvey, 1986)

Bibliography

Publications by John Ormond

Indications (with James Kirkup and John Bayliss). London: Grey Walls Press, 1943

Introduction to Dylan Thomas: *The Doctor and the Devils*. New York: Time, 1964, xiii-xix

Requiem and Celebration. Swansea: Christopher Davies, 1969

Corgi Modern Poets in Focus 5 (with Ezra Pound, Thom Gunn, Bernard Spencer, Sylvia Plath and Fleur Adcock) ed. Dannie Abse. London: Corgi Books, 1973

Definition of a Waterfall. London: Oxford University Press, 1973

Penguin Modern Poets 27 (with Emyr Humphreys and John Tripp). Harmondsworth: Penguin, 1979

Graham Sutherland, O.M.: A Memorial Address. Cardiff: National Museum of Wales, 1981

In place of an empty heaven: the poetry of Wallace Stevens. (W.D. Thomas Memorial Lecture, 7 December 1982) : Swansea: University College of Swansea, 1983

Selected Poems. Bridgend: Poetry Wales Press, 1987

Introduction to John Tripp: *Selected Poems* ed. John Ormond. Bridgend: Seren Books, 1989, 9-13

Cathedral Builders and Other Poems (with line-drawings by the author). Newtown: Gwasg Gregynog, 1991

Boundaries and other Poems. The Corgi Series: Writing from Wales 19. ed. Meic Stephens with his introduction. Llanrwst: Gwasg Carreg Gwalch, 2004

Borrowed Pasture: Notes on a Film. Journal of Film and Television Arts. Summer 1961, 6-8

Horizons Hung in Air: Kyffin Williams. London Welshman, November 1966, 7-9

A Music Restored: review of *Selected Stories* by Glyn Jones, *Planet 7*, 1971, 3-11

R.S. Thomas, priest and poet [transcript of Ormond's BBC film, broadcast 2 April 1972, with introduction by Sam Adams]. *Poetry Wales 7/4* (1972), 47-57

"Ceri Richards: Root and Branch". *Planet 10* (1972), 3-11

Ceri Richards. [Catalogue essay for the Ceri Richards Memorial Exhibition, Cardiff]. National Museum of Wales. 1973, 7-11

John Ormond: an autobiographical essay in 25 points. *Artists in Wales 2* ed. Meic Stephens. Llandysul: Gwasg Gomer, 1973, 155-64
"Gwyn Thomas" *Contemporary Novelists of the English Language* ed. James Vinson. London: St. James's Press, 1976, 1360-2
In Certain Lights [Extracts from a work in progress] *Planet 36* (1966), 37-39
"An ABC of Dannie Abse." *The Poetry of Dannie Abse* ed. Joseph Cohen. London: Robson Books, 1983, 108-35
"There you are, he's an artist" *Ceri Richards* [An Exhibition to inaugurate the Ceri Richards Gallery at The Taliesin Centre]. Swansea: University College of Swansea, (1984) 22-4
Introduction to *Kyffin Williams*, R.A.: A Catalogue for a Retrospective Exhibition. Cardiff: National Museum of Wales, 1987, 10-27
"Picturegoers" (1980) and "Selected Poems" (1987) *Wales on the Wireless: A Broadcasting Anthology* ed. Patrick Hannan. Llandysul: Gomer, 1988, 58-60; 166-8
"Letter from Tuscany" *Poetry Wales 24/1* (1988) 20-4
"Beginnings" *Wales in Vision* ed. Patrick Hannan. Llandysul: Gomer, 1990, 1-10

About John Ormond

Abse, Dannie. "John Ormond as Portraitist." *Poetry Wales 26/2* (1990), 5-7
——————— "In Llandaff Cathedral." *Goodbye Twentieth Century*. London: Pimlico, 2001, 281-7
——————— "John Ormond, a Neglected Poet." *The Two Roads Taken*. London: Enitharmon Press, 2003, 153-9 (Revised version of the introduction from *Corgi Modern Poets in Focus* 5)
Adams, Sam. "Quartet: Four Poets from the Early Years of *Poetry Wales.*" *Poetry Wales 40/1* (2004), 54-60
Berry, David. *Wales and Cinema: the First Hundred Years*. Cardiff: University of Wales Press, 1994, 282-5, 290-97
Berry, Ron. "What comes after?" *Poetry Wales 27/3* (1990), 54-5
Berthoud, Roger. *Graham Sutherland: A Biography*. London: Faber and Faber, 1982, 298, 305
Brown, Tony. "At the utmost edge: the poetry of John Ormond." *Poetry Wales 27/3* (1990), 31-6

Collins, Michael J. "The Anglo-Welsh poet John Ormond." *World Literature Today 51* (1977), 534-7

————————— "The elegiac tradition in contemporary Anglo-Welsh poetry. *Anglo-Welsh Review 76* (1984) 46-57

————————— "John Ormond" in The poets of Great Britain and Ireland, 1945-1960, *Dictionary of Literary Biography 27* ed. Vincent B. Sherry, Jr. Detroit: Gale Research Company, 1984, 269-75

————————— "Craftsmanship as meaning: the poetry of John Ormond." *Poetry Wales 16/2*, (1980), 25-33.

————————— "The gift of John Ormond." *Poetry Wales 27/3* (1990), 4-8

————————— "John Ormond in Tuscany." *Poetry Wales 35/4* (2000) 15-19

Curtis, Tony. "Grafting the sour to sweetness: Anglo-Welsh poetry in the last twenty-five years." *Wales: The Imagined Nation: Studies in Cultural and National Identity* ed. Tony Curtis. Bridgend: Poetry Wales Press, 1986, 99-126

Davies, James A. "Detached Attachment." *New Welsh Review 10:3* (1997-98), 37-9.

Felton, Mick. Review of *Cathedral Builders and other Poems. Poetry Wales 27/3* (1990) 62-3

Garlick, Raymond. "A Gregynog cathedral." Review of *Cathedral Builders and other Poems. Planet 89* (1991) 93-94

Harris, John. "John Ormond." *A Bibliographical Guide to Twenty-Four Modern Anglo-Welsh Writers.* Cardiff: University of Wales Press, 1994

Hooker, Jeremy. "The accessible song: a study of John Ormond's recent poetry." *The Anglo-Welsh Review 23* (1974), 5-12. Reprinted in Hooker, *The Presence of the Past: Essays on Modern British and American Poetry.* Bridgend: Poetry Wales Press, 1987, 106-13

Hopkinson, Tom. *Of This Our Time: a journalist's story* 1905-1950. London: Hutchinson, 1982, 236-7, 286

Jenkins, Randal. "The poetry of John Ormond." *Poetry Wales 8/1* (1972) 17-28

Jones, Glyn. "Poetry at the Casson: 'Womb to tomb' and 'Timeslip'" On poetry readings by John Ormond and Leslie Norris. *Anglo-Welsh Review 49* (1973), 107-113

Jones, Glyn. "John Ormond 1923-1990." *Poetry Wales 26/2* (1990) 3-5

Jones, Daniel. *My Friend, Dylan Thomas.* London: J.M. Dent & Sons, 1977.

Maud, Ralph (ed.) *Wales in his arms: Dylan Thomas's choice of Welsh poetry*. Cardiff: University of Wales Press, 1994.

Minhinnick, Robert. "The echo of once being here: a reflection on the imagery of John Ormond." *Poetry Wales 27/3* (1990), 51-3

———————— "The Sunflower" in *Island of Lightning*. Bridgend: Poetry Wales Press, 2013

O'Neill, Christopher. "Notes towards a bibliography of John Ormond's works." *Poetry Wales 16/2* (1980), 34-8

Ormond, Glenys. "'J.O.' and 'Rod'." *Poetry Wales 27/3* (1990), 42-5

Norris, Leslie. Review of Requiem and Celebration. *Poetry Wales 5* (1969) 47-53

Poole, Richard. "The voices of John Ormond." *Poetry Wales 16/2*, 12-24

———————— Review of *Selected Poems. Poetry Wales 23/1*, (1988), 62-4

———————— "Conversations with John Ormond." *The New Welsh Review 2:1* (1989), 39-46

———————— "John Ormond and Wallace Stevens: six variations on a double theme." *Poetry Wales 27/3* (1990), 16-26

Smith, David (Dai). "A cannon off the cush." *Arcade*, 18 November 1980, 13-14

Smith, Kieron. "John Ormond: Poetry, Broadcasting and Film." *New Welsh Review 95*, (2012)

———————— John Ormond and the BBC Wales Film Unit: Poetry, Documentary, Nation (unpublished doctoral thesis, Swansea University, 2014)

Swallow, Norman. *Factual Television*. London: Focal Press, 1966.

Thomas, Rian Ormond (Rian Evans). Introduction to *Cathedral Builders and Other Poems*. Newtown: Gwasg Gregynog, 1991, vii-x

Thomas, M. Wynn. John Ormond. *Writers of Wales*. Cardiff: University of Wales Press, 1997

Trayler-Smith, Richard *In requiem and celebration*. BBC 1995.

Walters, Gwyn. "The early John Ormond: a tribute." *The New Welsh Review 3:1* (1990) 27

Index of titles

Index of first lines

Acknowledgements

My father was grateful for the support of *Poetry Wales* and its various editors, of whom Meic Stephens was the first. In thanking them, I must record my own gratitude to Cary Archard whose encouragement of this present venture was crucial. I would also like to extend thanks to Michael Collins for his loyal championing of my father's work over the years and, similarly, to Robert Williams without whose generosity the Cortona connection would not have been so fruitful.

There are many friends to whom I am indebted for their help and perception: James Bradfield, Andrew Clements, Elizabeth Pengilly and Nicholas Sinclair, together with all those whose general chivvying was invaluable. Instrumental in the process was my late uncle, W.W. Roderick, but my whole family – John Ormond's family – has been brilliant. Finally, I would like to express my deep appreciation of Patrick McGuinness's contribution, not simply for his introduction but for his advice. And to Mick Felton my warm thanks for his patience.

Rian Evans